George Wilson Booth

Personal Reminiscences of a Maryland Soldier in the War between the States

1861-1865

George Wilson Booth

Personal Reminiscences of a Maryland Soldier in the War between the States
1861-1865

ISBN/EAN: 9783337307127

Printed in Europe, USA, Canada, Australia, Japan

Cover: Foto ©ninafisch / pixelio.de

More available books at **www.hansebooks.com**

Personal Reminiscences

OF A

Maryland Soldier

IN THE

War Between the States,

1861-1865.

FOR PRIVATE CIRCULATION ONLY.

BALTIMORE.
1898.

1861.

1861.

At the request of somewhat partial friends, I have undertaken to write out some of the events which came under my personal observation during the great struggle which convulsed our country, now more than a third of a century ago. The narrative must of necessity be more or less personal in its character, and may offend the sensibilities of some readers, while it will doubtless do violence to my own sense of modesty; but one cannot very well speak of the things he saw or did without this peculiarity, which is here stated at the outset, to break as far as possible the effect of this disagreeable feature.

My early predilections were of a martial character. As a boy, the story of the deeds of soldier and sailor were to me of the most engrossing interest, and the display of heroism which attended the long struggle of the Revolutionary period, the war of 1812, and later, that with Mexico, were cherished in my youthful recollections and read and reread with an ardor that almost approached worship. As soon as my years warranted, I became a member of the State volunteer soldiery in an organization of considerable reputation, the Independent Greys of Baltimore, and acquired a fair proficiency in the elementary work of a soldier, the manual of arms and the school of the company.

My early reading and associations led me to take views of the great questions which agitated and disturbed the public mind, in the days of 1860, by enlisting most strongly my sympathies in favor of the rights of the States under the constitution, and in opposition to efforts and the dominant purpose of the north to violate the express terms of that compact, and to destroy the principles of home government. With all this, in common with most Marylanders, was held in sacred reverence the love of the Union and the glories of our common country. The dissolution of the Union was looked upon as a threatened evil, to be averted by mutual concession and forbearance, and the efforts of those patriotic statesmen who so earnestly strove to prevent this dire calamity found in my heart a most responsive sentiment. After the lapse of many years, during which the crude thoughts and convictions of these earlier days have matured in character and strength, and in the judgment which comes after experience, having been sanctified by trial and suffering, it is in no sense of vainglory or boasting that I solemnly record that my mind and heart the more strongly justify the views of my youth, and my only regret is, that my slender abilities did not permit me to be more efficient in the defense of those principles which are the very foundation and bulwark of a State, whose chief glory and power comes from a government with the consent of its people.

With the greatest regard for truthfulness, I can say that never for one moment did the question of slavery or the perpetuation of that institution enter into the decision of my course. When the first blow was struck at Sumter, and men were forced to take sides in the approaching conflict, that which impelled to decision was the love of freedom, and the constitution of my country, as I understood it, as opposed to the vindictiveness of the northern politician and his hatred of our southern brethren, as evidenced in the disregard of public faith and the coercive measures which were being set on foot to bring them under the rod.

As a member of the military force of the State, I promptly responded to the call to arms, to maintain the public peace, and to prevent the passage of northern troops through its territory, and when the efforts of our authorities became futile, and their functions were usurped by the federal government; when it became apparent, without question, that the hope of State action was impracticable, by reason of this military occupation, then, without hesitation, I chose to cast my fortune with the south and to bear a part in the great struggle.

My first experience under fire was on Pratt street, Baltimore, April 19th, 1861, on the occasion of the passage of the 6th Massachusetts regiment. The fall of Sumter was immediately followed by the call of Mr. Lincoln for troops, and the States of the north hastened forward their quotas to Washington.

The public mind in Baltimore was in a state of intense excitement, and it only required a little friction to cause an explosion. Several bodies of troops had passed through the city, when, on the morning of April 19th, there arrived at Baltimore the above-named regiment. Transfer between the Philadelphia and the Washington depots was made in those days by hauling the cars along Pratt street by horse-power. A number of these cars, filled with soldiers, went through without any other notice except the jeering of the people, but finally the passions of the crowd led to more pronounced action, and when, just before noon, moved by curiosity and interest in what was transpiring, I reached the corner of Gay and Pratt streets, the explosion had occurred. The people, who appeared to be without organization or leadership, had barricaded the tracks by emptying thereon loads of sand from passing carts, and by dragging some old anchors and chains from a ship chandlery establishment on the corner. A car had reached the obstructed point, and, not being able to pass, the horses were attached to the rear and the car was being returned to the Philadelphia depot. During this movement the soldiers in the car were subjected to the most violent abuse, and occasionally stones were hurled into the doors and windows. The portion of the regiment thus cut off was then formed in the street, and the march for Camden Station commenced.

These events had drawn to Pratt street a large number of people, who lined the sidewalks and followed the movement of the troops. I was standing at the corner of Commerce street and the troops were at the moment passing that point, when a soldier, struck by a stone, fell almost at my feet, and as he fell, dropped his musket, which was immediately seized by a citizen, who raised it to his shoulder and fired into the column. The rear files faced about and delivered a volley into the crowd, who responded with pistol shots, stones, clubs and other missiles. A perfect fusilade for the next few blocks was kept up between the troops and the enraged mob, the troops taking the double quick and the crowd closely following. As the Maltby House was reached, the police, under the Mayor and Marshal, intervened between the flying soldiers and their pursuers, the remainder of the march to Camden Station being made comparatively in good order and free from molestation.

The dead and wounded soldiers and citizens lying in the street were looked after, while the excitement grew every moment, until the alarm was sounded from the town bells and the military assembled. Within an hour the military was moved to Monument Square and held awaiting orders.

I am very frank to say that when the firing commenced, being in the very midst of it, I quickly realized my danger and was convinced that I was entirely out of place. I had no weapon save a penknife, and nothing in the line of destruction except a few musket cartridges, which were in my pocket by reason of service on guard at the armory the night previous.

I knew very well, by sight, the man who picked up the musket and fired the first shot, but did not then know his name. As he fired he turned and asked if anyone had a cartridge. I gave him one or two and showed him how to reload, then betook myself to the protection of the first doorway, thus escaping the bullets which were sweeping the street. Later on, this same party enlisted in my company, and I learned to know him well. Although advanced in years, he bore the fatigues of the march and the duties of the camp without murmuring. He was a true gentleman, who displayed his nobility of character in all the trials which he encountered, winning the respect and affection of all with whom he came in contact, and when, on June 6th, 1862, he yielded up his life in battle, near Harrisonburg, the cause of the Confederacy lost one of its most devoted and truest supporters.

For some ten days the Maryland military held Baltimore, destroying the bridges on the lines of railroad approaching the city from the north.

In the meantime the northern troops made their way to

Washington via Annapolis, and finally occupied the Relay, within nine miles of the city. The Maryland militia was then disbanded, and very soon Baltimore and the entire State were in possession of the federal power. Being invited by James R. Herbert to unite with him in raising a company for service in the southern army, and all prospect or opportunity for action on the part of the State having passed, this work for some time received my attention.

About the middle of May, 1861, a sufficient number of men to establish a nucleus for a company having been enlisted, Captain Herbert took his departure for Harper's Ferry, marching across the country and taking the train at Sykesville, on the B. & O. R. R., while I remained in Baltimore, forwarding daily additional men, until it became unsafe to linger longer, as arrests were being freely made by the federal authorities, and on Saturday, May 18th, I took the train for Harper's Ferry. Owing to the inspection of the federal guards, it was not practicable to take any equipment or baggage, so that when I landed at the Ferry that afternoon, I had nothing but the clothes on my back. The next few days were spent in organizing, and on May 22d, we were mustered into the service of the Confederate States, with James R. Herbert as Captain and myself as 2d Lieutenant, together with some sixty men, and became D company of the 1st Maryland regiment, with Arnold Elzey as Colonel, George H. Steuart as Lieutenant-Colonel and Bradley T. Johnson as Major. By the close of the month we mustered some eighty men, and I was made 1st Lieutenant, with William Key Howard and Nicholas Snowden as 2d Lieutenants. My experience with the "Greys" now served an excellent purpose, and in a little while, by unremitting drill and care, the company became proficient in drill and attracted attention. It was drill, drill from early morn to night.

The first person of distinction I remember, after reaching Harper's Ferry, was Col. T. J. Jackson, afterwards the immortal "Stonewall," who was in command of the post. I recall him as he rode down the hilly street, with his Virginia Military Institute cadet cap over his eyes, mounted on a rather small sorrel horse, riding with very short stirrups, knees bent and presenting altogether not a very martial figure. I remember Col. A. P. Hill as he drilled his regiment, the 13th Virginia, which included a company made up almost entirely of Baltimoreans. The most picturesque soldiers were the Kentuckians under Col. Blanton Duncan, who occupied the Maryland Heights. Their uniform was after the frontier hunting pattern, fancifully trimmed and very attractive; most conspicuous in their equipment was the "bowie."

Several Virginia regiments were neatly uniformed in grey, while the arriving troops from the more remote south were clad in the homespun butternut suits, soon to be so familiar. These troops came to the front with the most extensive paraphernalia, huge camp chests filled with all the service necessary for the mess; many of the privates brought with them their personal servants, while the officers were equipped with all that was necessary for elaborate entertainment. The camp equipment of one of these regiments called for as much wagon transportation as would have been accorded a division later on, when the army was on the march and in active service. The Maryland regiment numbered about 700 men, without uniform and without equipment; they stood in their "boots." Worse than this, the arms issued us were the old flint-lock musket type, which had been altered to percussion.

Not a cartridge box was in the command, and, taken altogether, we presented a sorry sight as compared with troops of other States. Relief from this unfavorable condition was brought about through the personal efforts of a noble woman, Mrs. Bradley T. Johnson, who interceded with Governor Ellis, of North Carolina, with such success as to secure some 600 Mississippi rifles, an excellent arm for those days, and by the purchase in Richmond of uniforms and clothing, which made us presentable. Shortly after the first of June some effort was made to organize the troops into brigades, and Colonel Jackson was made Brigadier-General of the 1st Virginia brigade, soon to be known as the famous "Stonewall Brigade" of the Army of Northern Virginia.

The command of the "Army of the Shenandoah," as it was officially designated, was assumed at this time by Brig.-Gen. Joseph E. Johnston. In the meantime, the federals were gathering their hosts in upper Maryland, under General Patterson, who moved in the direction of Williamsport, threatening to cross the river. General Johnston, therefore, determined to evacuate Harper's Ferry, and moved to interpose his force between Winchester and Patterson's advancing column. At Bunker Hill, a hamlet about midway between Winchester and Martinsburg, Johnston took position, and for two days we stood in line of battle. I suppose we fared as the rest when some twenty rounds of cartridges per man were distributed, with which we were expected to deliver the approaching battle. In the absence of cartridge and cap boxes, the cartridges and caps were conveyed to our pockets.

Patterson crossed the river and advanced to Martinsburg, when, being opposed by General Jackson, he concluded to return to Maryland, General Johnston retiring to a position in the vicinity of Winchester, holding the fords on the Potomac with a few cavalry.

At Winchester the regiment received numerous accessions, principally two companies, under Captains E. R. Dorsey and W. H. Murray, who had been mustered into the service at Richmond. These companies were armed with the improved Springfield musket, well uniformed and otherwise equipped. This gave us two companies with muskets and bayonets—our "Grenadiers," as we termed them, the remainder of the regiment being armed with the Mississippi rifle. While we lay at Winchester we made our first expedition. It appears that on the evacuation of Harper's Ferry, where the United States Government had extensive armories and rifle works, some portion had not been destroyed and there remained intact valuable machinery and quite a number of rifle stocks. Lieutenant-Colonel Steuart was directed to take the 1st Maryland and endeavor to secure and bring off this material. The regiment moved on train as far as Halltown, where it debarked and marched to the scene of operation and executed its mission with great success, returning to Winchester without loss. For this service General Johnston published in general orders his thanks to Colonel Steuart and his command. Before the regiment had been in service thirty days, it had won by its conduct the public approval and commendation of the commanding General. I was not so well satisfied with my participation, for the reason that, on reaching Halltown, I had been detached with some twenty or twenty-five men to hold the train while the regiment moved forward to Harper's Ferry. On expressing to Colonel Steuart my dissatisfaction at this arrangement, he was good enough to explain that he had assigned me to the post of honor, and that the safety of the command, in the protection of the means of returning from the presence of the enemy, depended on the faithfulness with which I kept my trust. This to me was a new view of the status, and my disappointment and mortification were dispelled. It was very kind in the Colonel to honor so youthful an officer, and I verily believe my stature increased several inches on his explanation. Afterwards, I do not think I took quite so much stock in my distinguished service on that occasion.

It was my fortune in these early days of the war to receive the appreciation and friendship of my commanding officers. Colonel Steuart, from the very first, took quite a fancy to me, and to this partiality I owe very much of the opportunity for familiarizing myself with the duties of a soldier.

The training and instruction received from this well-equipped and thorough soldier fitted me to discharge the important duties which afterwards I was called upon to assume, with at least a moderate measure of efficiency. Had I proved a better and a more appreciative scholar, my record would have been beyond doubt more satisfactory. There were but few officers, in either the confederate or federal service, who had the tact for organization and of military detail to the same degree as Col. George H. Steuart. The regiment, under his master hand, soon gave evidence of the soldierly qualities which made it the pride of the army and placed the fame of Maryland in the very foreground among the Southern States. As a disciplinarian he was most exacting, albeit not unkind. In his supervision of his men, in the way of instruction and in providing for their material wants, he was untiring. A terror to the evil-doer, he won the respect and ultimately the affection of his command. His assistant and next in rank, Lieut.-Col. Bradley T. Johnson, was to me more like an elder brother, and the friendship and love which have characterized our intercourse from our first acquaintance have been to me one of the sweetest episodes of a not altogether uneventful life.

This distinguished gentleman, although not equipped with the technical knowledge and military education of Colonel Steuart, soon became prominent by reason of his great force of character, his intimate knowledge of men and the great questions which were then determining the events of the period, and these qualifications, supplemented by his intelligent devotion to his State and the cause, and his pronounced personal gallantry in the field, made him the ideal Maryland soldier in the south, and as such he stood as the representative man from his State.

With the distinguished leadership of these officers, it is readily understood why the *morale* of the 1st Maryland regiment was of so high an order and their record as soldiers so brilliant.

Colonel Elzey did not serve in command of the regiment long enough to impress his personality upon its features; promotion took him to higher and wider fields, where he won distinction, both as a Brigade and later as a Department commander.

My personal relations with my commanding officers gave me opportunities for intelligent observation and knowledge of the movements of the army and the purposes of the campaign, far beyond those that fell ordinarily to one of my years or rank, and it is in recognition of this circumstance, that I have been sought by friends to write these reminiscences, and have felt it somewhat of a duty to my comrades that I should, in even so feeble a manner, respond to the call.

During the latter part of June and the early days of July, 1861, the army under General Johnston camped in the vicinity of Winchester, gaining in strength and efficiency, until the advance of McDowell from Washington on Beauregard, who held the lines on Bull Run, near Manassas, made it necessary for the former to move to the assistance of the threatened confederates. The troops were put in motion on the afternoon of July 18th, and after marching a few miles from the town, were halted, while the order of the day, announcing the attack on Beauregard's lines was read.

Stimulated by the enthusiasm which marked the publication of this information, the march was prolonged during the night, until early dawn found us at the crossing of the Shenandoah on the road leading through Paris to Piedmont, a station on the Manassas Gap Railroad. Before crossing the river, Colonel Steuart detached me from my own company and placed me in command of company F—Capt. J. Louis Smith, of this company, was disabled by sickness, and the other officers had fallen under the Colonel's displeasure and were under arrest. It was, therefore, my great honor to command this fine company from this point, through the great battle of July 21st and until Captain Smith was able to report again for duty. I lacked a few days of being seventeen years of age, and the responsibility of this assignment was a severe tax on my endurance. The men were entire strangers to me and I knew the names of but one or two of them. They were mostly of Irish-American descent, somewhat unruly, by reason of imperfect handling, but were of the material that makes the best of soldiers, and after the battle I had no further trouble with them. On the contrary, they appeared anxious to please their youthful commander, and the manifestation of affection and respect which came with this short association followed me the remaining days of the war, and I never lacked a friend when an old company F man was around.

Manassas was our "baptism of fire." On arrival at the Junction, about noon, on this eventful day, we were hurried towards the field, the booming of the cannon and the rattle of the musketry in the distance giving us notice of the stern work that was going on at the front. The heat was intense and the dust almost suffocating, and the march was most rapid, at times in a double quick. Gen. E. Kirby Smith assumed command of the brigade as we left the cars, and rode at the head of the column, which was made up of the 1st Maryland, the 10th Virginia and the 3d Tennessee, the remaining regiment, the 13th Virginia, Col. A. P. Hill, not having arrived when we started on our march. As we approached the field all the circumstantial attendants of battle were in evidence—the wounded were being brought out, the skulkers were in force with their tales of carnage and woe—"the day had gone against us," everybody was "cut up," and we were about to offer ourselves additional victims to the Moloch of destruction. Truly the rear of an army in battle is a point of great disadvantage to form a correct idea of the great deeds or gallant heroism of the men at the front, and to untried troops such as we were the experience was most trying and dispiriting. Yet no halt was made until a sharp volley of musketry into the head of our column announced we had reached the scene of conflict. Under this fire, poured into us as we were marching in column, General Smith fell from his horse, badly wounded, and a number of our men were similarly disabled. Then came a halt for a moment, and the order was passed down the line to "lie down." This to my untutored mind was so repugnant to the preconceived ideas of a soldier's behavior in battle, that, while I passed the order to the men I remained standing, looking around to see from whence came the destroying messengers.

My education in this particular was very rapid and thorough, and to "lie down" or to "hug dirt," as the boys termed it, soon became a movement in tactics with which I became familiar, and, with becoming modesty, may add, in which I became something of an expert. In fact, the presentation of these pages is a forcible exemplification of the poetic truth that "he who fights and runs away may live to fight another day."

Colonel Elzey had very much resented the command of the brigade passing to General Smith, and, on the disablement of the latter, again assumed command, with some pious ejaculations as to the "justice" of Providence, and it becoming apparent that his correct position was somewhat further to the left, rapidly moved in that direction and then formed his line of battle. After advancing a short distance through a body of timber, as we approached the edge of the woods, there was before us a small clearing, rising from which was a hill just opposite our line, and on this high ground was a considerable body of troops massed, just in the act of deploying. Although at no great distance, we could not make out their identity satisfactorily. Their uniforms were grey, and their colors hung closely to the color-staff, while the smoke from the field made the atmosphere something of a light fog and rendered objects not immediately at hand more or less indistinct. In a moment, however, a faint breeze came along, and under its influence the colors spread out before us—the stars and stripes—the "d—d old gridiron," Elzey exclaimed, and thus assured, gave the order to fire. The Colonel was immediately in rear of my company at this time, and as soon as he gave the word, I passed the order to my men and the line from right to left blazed out in a succession of volleys, of a character so destructive as to throw the force in our front into disorder and then retreat. The order to charge was then given, and we went after them with a will. The enemy made attempt to rally and stop our advance, but we had them at such disadvantage, and their loss was so considerable, that they were unable to break our charge, which continued until we reached the high ground, when before us was the battlefield as a panorama. At this juncture, still further to our left, a confederate battery opened on the flying federal masses, and then appeared a body of confederate infantry moving forward, taking the federal right in flank. To our right our troops had just driven back the federal attack, and under these combined circumstances and the immediate advance of our lines, the federal host gave way all along the lines and made for the crossings at the Stone Bridge and above that point in a disorder which soon became a panic, and the discomfiture was complete. Our troops pressed forward to the position occupied by the enemy amidst the wildest cheering and enthusiasm, which was heightened by the appearance of President Davis, together with Generals Johnston and Beauregard, as they rode over the field and among the troops. It was a glorious moment for the southern soldier—victory was snatched from defeat and our enemy was flying before us. The captured guns were the objects of great interest, while the many prisoners, who were being carried back, added to the evidences of victory. The federal rout continued until the very defenses of Washington were reached, and many did not stay their flight until in the streets of the Capital they laid their wearied forms to seek rest. The confederate pursuit did not extend beyond Bull Run, except that a few companies of cavalry followed the flying mob to within a short distance of Centreville, where the federal reserve was in position.

The scarcity of cavalry prevented a more vigorous pursuit, and our generals were not fully informed as to the extent of the federal disaster until the following day. As an evidence of this, we marched that night from the Stone Bridge to a point on the old Orange & Alexandria Railroad, just in rear of Union Mills, a distance of some eight miles, to be in position to meet the expected advance of the enemy the next day. By the next morning there was no organized body of the enemy nearer than the defenses around Alexandria.

Before dawn on the morning of the 23d, Col. J. E. B. Stuart, with some cavalry and the Maryland regiment, moved in the direction of Centreville. After fording Bull Run, which was very high by reason of the heavy rains of the 22d, we came upon the evidences of the rout; the roads were strewn with all sorts of material—arms, clothing, stores and wagons—which had been abandoned in the mad flight of the army, which had but a few days previously passed along with banners flying and music playing to enliven their "onward to Richmond." On reaching Fairfax Court House our command was camped, and within the next few days the army occupied this line and we were moved to the railroad at Fairfax Station, in which camp we passed several months, and then were retired to the Centreville lines, where we remained until going into winter quarters on the approach of cold weather. These months, from July to December, were spent in perfecting the organization of the army and in the drill of the troops—company drill, battalion drill, brigade drill, and occasionally we attempted the maneuvers of the division. The tedium of these autumn days was sensibly relieved by occasional tours at the outposts in the vicinity of Mason's and Upton's hills, in sight of the dome of the Capitol, with an expedition to the vicinity of Pohick church and occasional skirmishes with the enemy on their outposts or advanced lines. Meanwhile the army grew in numbers and in efficiency, if not in contentment.

In describing a military condition, under somewhat similar circumstances, an old writer says "the army swore in Flanders." Truly did the confederate army swear around Centreville. The policy which determined this prolonged inaction was canvassed and criticised most freely. The brilliant success of July 21st, it was held, called for immediate and vigorous advance, and our rank and file were unsparing in their condemnation of this supineness. It was said Jackson wanted to advance, that Johnston and Beauregard disagreed, and then that Mr. Davis had overruled these commanders. The amount of military wisdom that was displayed and eloquence that was expended in these camp-fire discussions was convincing at least of one fact—that talent for command was not altogether confined to the general officers—very much after the manner of General Lee in later years, in reading the scathing criticisms of the newspaper editors in their reviews of the movements in the field, when he gave utterance to the thought that, after all, perhaps, he had made a great mistake and his services might be more profitably utilized to the country by publishing a newspaper, while these knights of quill and scissors had an opportunity to make effective their military talents and genius in directing the operations of the army.

The truth was, the leaders on both sides had learned this lesson at Manassas—the war was not to be a summer episode to be determined in a few days or months; that before us, in all its hideousness, was the spectre of a prolonged, bitter and bloody struggle, the result of which depended on armies of trained soldiers and not of armed mobs. To meet this requirement it was necessary to perfect organization, and the federal authorities appear to have reached this conclusion with greater directness, and made effective the theory, in advance of ourselves.

The confederate situation was very soon confronted with the difficulties which followed the hasty and ill-advised manner in which troops had been brought into the field. The want of proper officers now became painfully manifest. The meagre equipment and its poverty-stricken character presented a problem that was positively discouraging to consider, and to make the cup of misery overflow, came sickness and disease, which distressingly developed the incapacity of our organization to properly care for the men. Regiments which had come to the front, 1000 strong, were reduced to the number of a company by measles, mumps, chicken-pox and such kindred disorders. The enthusiasm of the early volunteer gave way under these trials, and as the terms of enlistment for the short periods for which the troops were at first taken into service neared expiration, the army approached the verge of disintegration. This situation prevailed when the army moved into winter quarters, but from which it emerged in the following spring. purified as by fire, to attempt the deeds which now stand before an admiring world as an exhibition of as high a character of martial prowess and endurance as ever witnessed.

Our regiment was measurably free from these troubles. The men were largely drawn from city life or the better classes of the country population. There was more life and spirit in the average Maryland soldier than in a score of those from the interior of some of the Southern States. The magnificent work of Colonel Steuart made his camps healthful and free from disease. He was a foe to idleness, and kept his men always on the alert, and under his careful administration wastefulness was not permitted, and the greatest of comfort was extracted from every advantage. He made his men proud of their command, and it was no unusual sight to have thousands from the surrounding camps flock to the roadside, as the Marylanders marched out to or returned from some tour of duty. No matter how fatigued the men were from the long march, as the camps of the army were neared, the drum corps would beat its stirring march and the files would be closed up, as, with quick step and jaunty air, they swung along, the observed of all observers. We had, too, our jokes on the Colonel. Who does not recall the mysterious grand rounds made in the dead hour of the night, when the poor unsuspecting sentry or guard was pounced upon, with his cry of "Indians! Indians!" Who has forgotten the "pen," with its attendant shower-bath, which roused to sensibility the unfortunate who had succumbed to the "wine when it was red" and found himself incarcerated in its inhospitable confines? Who remembers not, as yesterday, the steady pace with which the offender and violator of orders perambulated before the Colonel's quarters, carrying a fence rail or other burden, under the watchful eye of a guard? Even now, I can almost imagine my olfactories have wafted to them odors of the decaying goose, which the lover of "fowl" deeds carried suspended to his neck, displaying for several days, in the sickening heat of a September sun, the evidence of his guilt, as a warning to others evilly inclined.

Shortly after reaching Fairfax Court House I was disabled by a severe attack of bilious fever, and it was determined to send me to hospital. Now, there were two things above all others for which I had the greatest horror—going to a hospital and being taken prisoner. Against the former I protested and begged so piteously that permission was given to remain in camp, and under the skillful care of Drs. Galliard and Latimer, our surgeons, together with the kind and attentive ministrations of my comrades, I pulled through, although it was fully two months before I was fit for regular duty, but I escaped the hospital and was thankful. When the regiment moved I went with it; when not able to ride a horse, I rode in the ambulance, and as I gained in strength the Colonel assigned me to light duty at headquarters, and finally detached me from my company and made me Adjutant. In this capacity I served until near the close of the winter, when I secured a leave of absence for a few days and visited Richmond and Norfolk to obtain some necessary clothing, etc. This service as Adjutant with Colonel Steuart was of immense advantage to me in the way of education for the duties of an officer, but the labors were very exacting, and I never felt altogether satisfied to be away from my company, and Captain Herbert was not willing I should remain away from my duty with him. Again, the men frequently would ask me to come back, and, as I had enlisted many of them in Baltimore, I felt somewhat under obligation to stand by them; so when I reached Richmond on my leave, I wrote to Colonel Steuart requesting that, on my return, I be permitted to resume my company duties. To this he consented. After my convalescence from the fever, I had an enormous appetite and my physique developed most rapidly. This taking on of flesh did not favorably commend itself to the Colonel, and he frequently said to me: "Mr. Booth, you are getting too fat," and I verily believe he was to some degree moved to grant my petition by the circumstance that his Adjutant was losing the graceful proportions which, in his judgment, should adorn the holder of that important position. I do not know what he will say to the statement, but somehow I felt impressed ever afterward that I had fallen from grace in his eyes and that he never had the same interest in me after my return.

Whilst we were at Centreville, and during my turn as Adjutant, there came to us an Irishman by the name of Haffey, who gave out he had deserted from the U. S. Steamer Pawnee, which was then patrolling the Potomac near our lines at Occoquan. This man enlisted in one of the companies and was generally known as "Pawnee." He proved to be a fairly good soldier, but was experienced in ways that were not altogether in harmony with the Colonel's ideas of discipline, and, when in liquor, was a noisy, disagreeable subject to handle. During one of his drunken frolics he had been committed to the "pen" and was brought under the wholesome influences of the cold-water cure; but as the water was freely administered it failed in its usual efficacy, and drew from him but renewed abuse and violent rejoinder, "Pour on, d—n you"—"pour on"—together with other objurgations, offensive to ears polite. The Colonel then determined on other methods of treatment, and the poor half-drowned wretch was brought to his quarters and placed upon a large box, from which some clothing had just been distributed, a gag was placed in his mouth, which silenced his flow of vulgar obscenity and abuse, and then the "buck" applied. In this position, "bucked and gagged," this dilapidated warrior spent the better part of a day in deep disgrace, a monument of warning and mistaken zeal. In some unaccountable manner, however, he managed to release the buck, and, removing the gag from his mouth, he betook himself to more comfortable surroundings and localities. When it came to the Colonel's knowledge that "Pawnee" was gone, his indignation was profound, and the neglectful sentry was relieved from his post and summarily consigned to the "pen," where he could leisurely meditate upon the strange mutations of army life. Sending his orderly for me post haste, the Colonel exclaimed: "Mr. Booth, send the officer of the guard with a detachment through the camps and direct him to bring back the prisoner alive or dead." The officer of the guard that day was my dear friend, Nicholas Snowden, a Lieutenant in my own company, and as noble a soul as ever wore an uniform.

When I delivered to him the instruction, he turned to me in dismay: "In the name of God, how am I to find this man, whom I do not even know, in the camps of 20,000 men." This I well knew would not avail with the Colonel, so I advised Lieutenant Snowden to take his guard and go from the camp and make at least an ostensible effort to find and arrest the culprit. As a matter of course, after a few hours' search he returned without his prisoner, and report was made, the man had made good his escape. By this time the Colonel had exploded his superfluity of wrath and the guard was dismissed. The episode bid fair to be numbered with the past, when on the morning of the second day, as the Colonel emerged from his tent, whom should he see mounted on the same box, squatting in the position of the "buck," but the irrepressible "Pawnee," who, with smiling countenance, saluted him with "Good mornin', Colonel, good mornin' to ye." The humor of the situation overcame the sternness of discipline, and Haffey was directed to report to his company without further question or punishment.

Another incident I recall, which evidenced how discipline was tempered with justice. One of the most serious troubles we had to contend with was the difficulty to detail men for special duty in very necessary but not inviting fields, such as driving wagons and other duty in connection with the Quartermaster or Commissary Department. Our men, as a rule, had not left Maryland to drive wagons, yet it was just as important to have wagons and wagon drivers as it was to have soldiers in the ranks. Again, a number of our companies were made up of city-bred men, who were not proficient in the sublime art of handling with dexterity a four-mule team, even had they been so disposed, and this ungrateful task compelled frequent calls on those companies which were comprised largely of country boys and more competent for the purpose. On one occasion we were breaking camp near Centreville, when the Quartermaster reported he was short a wagon driver for Captain Murray's company wagon—in those days we rejoiced in a wagon to each company—and the Colonel directed me to detail a man for the purpose. As we were just about to march off, there was but little time or opportunity for diplomatic action in so grave a matter, and I turned at once to a source where wagon drivers were galore, and directed the Captain to send a man to the Quartermaster. Now, this Captain was then, and is today, one of my best and dearest friends. He was a soldier of the greatest gallantry and an officer of superior merit and ability. He was, however, not slow to wrath, and when he received my order, the recollections of previous frequent indignities and demands in this direction rose up before his angered vision, and in language most emphatic, if not extremely choice, he evidenced his disinclination to comply. Assuming he would think better of it in a few moments, I turned to other duties and the circumstance passed from my mind, when the Quartermaster put in another appearance and explained to the Colonel he had not moved off with his train for the reason he still was without a driver for this miserable wagon. This, of course, threw the responsibility upon me, and, muttering some excuse, I hastened back to my recalcitrant friend and again delivered the order, but with no better success. My own patience becoming somewhat tried, I was, perhaps, overzealous, but all I could get out of him was, "Tell Colonel Steuart I will see him d—d before I will furnish the wagon drivers for the regiment. You have already seven of my men; not another one can you have." My expostulations and representations, as to the peculiar and pressing character of the emergency, availed naught, and I finally was forced to say, "Well, Captain, if you mean that I shall carry your message to the Colonel I will do so *verbatim et literatim*," and off I went and made report.

"Arrest Captain —— at once and send a man to the wagon," was the Colonel's angry reply. Back again I went and urged compliance, before resorting to such extreme measures—visions of courts-martial before my eyes—but without result. My choleric friend still persisted in his disobedience and was placed in arrest, when I made demand on his 1st Lieutenant, now in command. This officer had the fear of his Captain before him, and, as the demand was made in his presence, he likewise refused compliance. I did not take the trouble to make further report, but at once arrested this officer and then turned to the remaining subaltern, whose fear of the displeasure of his own officers was fortunately less than that of the Colonel, and I got my man. In the course of the next day I took occasion to explain matters to the Colonel and urged him to oblige me by releasing the offending officers in view of their general good record and the peculiar circumstances and injustice which was being done them and their men. After some persuasion he consented, and what promised to be an affair disagreeable in consequences blew over without hurt.

Strange to say, in my after-experience in this matter of wagon drivers, the difficulty which was so aggravated in 1861 disappeared along about 1863, and in 1864 or 1865 I confidently aver such details were at a premium. It is wonderful how men and opinions change with time.

1862.

1862.

The winter of 1861 and 1862 was spent in quarters near Manassas, in comfortable huts, erected in what was a thick pine forest, but which succumbed to the axes of our men and soon developed into a miniature city, with regularly laid out streets and avenues. The regiment furnished its quota of pickets and outpost guards, and two companies were detailed under Lieutenant-Colonel Johnson, when, in the early part of March, 1862, the advance of McClellan was made, necessitating the withdrawal of the army, which was at that time much depleted and in process of reorganization, to the line of the Rappahannock. This movement determined McClellan to transfer the federal forces to the Peninsula and prosecute the "onward to Richmond" from that quarter. General Johnston rapidly moved to confront the enemy, leaving on the Rappahannock Ewell's Division, made up of the brigades of Elzey, Trimble and Richard Taylor, with instructions to keep in a position to support Jackson, who was resisting the advance of Banks in the Valley, or of the main army, below Richmond, as circumstances might require. In the discharge of this duty, and at the urgent call of General Jackson, about the first of May, we moved through Swift Run Gap, crossing the Blue Ridge mountains, and took position at Conrad's store on the Shenandoah. In descending the mountains on the night of our arrival, we viewed the camp fires of Jackson, and eagerly looked forward to the pleasure of meeting our old friends of the Stonewall brigade and the Marylanders, who, under Capt. Lyle Clarke, had been serving in Western Virginia, and who, we now supposed, were with Jackson. The battle of Kernstown had in the meantime been fought, and although our troops had been compelled to relinquish the field, the heroism there displayed and the far-reaching consequences of that well-contested field were familiar to us, and we longed to hear from our old comrades the story of their struggle. Tired and worn out by the fatigues of the march, we went into bivouac, full of anticipation for the morrow's reunion. When the morning came there was left nothing, save the smoldering embers of the camp fires of the previous night. Jackson had disappeared, whither, no one seemed to know. For some days we remained in this state of disappointment and uncertainty, which, singular to relate, was shared by General Ewell and his brigade commanders. It is said that General Ewell called a council of his Brigadiers and discussed with them the peculiar situation. Here he was with his division, without orders, without very much information as to the position or purposes of Banks, who was not very remote, and absolutely without any knowledge of the movements or whereabouts of General Jackson, and it was a serious question if his instructions from General Johnston did not require him to return to the east of the Blue Ridge. This movement was finally determined on, when the army was electrified by the notable dispatch from Jackson, "God blessed our arms with victory at McDowell yesterday." It is said that when this dispatch was received at the War Department, it required some investigation to locate where McDowell was situated. So well had the great leader concealed his movements that even his own superiors were not informed as to his operations. The federal commander, General Milroy, however, in a manner decidedly unpleasant, was enlightened on the subject, and also unfortunate enough to receive another like lesson about a year later, when Ewell introduced himself in the vicinity of Winchester.

 I remember distinctly, as if it were yesterday, when Jackson joined Ewell's division. We marched from the vicinity of Conrad's store and the head of the column recrossed the mountain and had about reached its eastern base; our regiment was just about the summit, when there came riding rapidly up the road, which was comparatively free from obstruction, as the column had been halted and the men were resting on the roadside, a mounted officer, with several attendants. As they neared the point where we were, it was at once discovered that *"Jackson"* had come, and the hearty shouting and cheers of the men re-echoed among the mountain tops. Enquiring for General Ewell, he pushed forward and in a little while returned with that officer, when right-about was the command, and we retraced our steps down the mountain and halted for the night on the road to Luray. The next morning the march was resumed, and on the morning of May 23d we reached Front Royal, which was occupied by a federal force, consisting of the 1st Maryland Infantry, two companies of Pennsylvania infantry and a portion of the 5th New York cavalry, with two guns of Knap's battery of artillery, aggregating about 1000 men, under command of Col. Jno. R. Kenly.

Within a few miles of Front Royal, General Jackson halted his army and directed Colonel Johnson to bring his regiment to the front. The regiment by this time had lost one company, by reason of expiration of terms of enlistment, and very great dissatisfaction existed in some of the remaining companies, who claimed their term of enlistment was but for twelve months, whereas the muster-rolls showed their period of service was "for the war." The feeling was quite bitter, and as the Colonel, supported by most of the officers, could not recognize the claim of the men in face of facts as shown by the muster-rolls, and very vigorously denounced the agitators, it was apparent that the usual discipline had given way and a spirit of insubordination was rife. On the 22d of May, quite a number of men refused to perform duty, were disarmed and marched in the rear of the regiment under arrest. The entire strength of the regiment at this time was not more than 350 men present for duty, and not more than 250 of these could be counted upon by reason of the lamentable condition in which we were when Jackson's order to come to the front was received. Colonel Johnson, however, rose to the situation, and in an address to the men he pictured the shame that would be theirs, and the dishonor to the State, if they failed to respond. Most scathing in his denunciation, and yet most fervent in his appeals to preserve the reputation of Maryland, his few words have been remembered by me as the most effective eloquence to which it has been my fortune to listen. Judged by the result, it transformed a body of sullen, angry and discontented men to enthusiastic, obedient soldiers, anxious to be led to the fray. "Give us back our guns and we will show you if Maryland is to be put to shame," was their response. In a few moments the disarmed men were re-equipped, when, with colors flying and with quick step, we marched through the halted columns amid the cheers and plaudits of the troops, who knew nothing of the events which had so dangerously threatened our fair fame. After a march of a few miles we struck the outposts, which were driven in at once and several prisoners made, then it was we learned that our antagonists were the 1st Maryland federal regiment. The effect of the information was of varied character. We were about to meet in conflict many of our former friends, perhaps in some cases our kinsmen, for Kenly's regiment was largely made up of Baltimoreans. To some this was a sorrow, to others the passions of the times made the encounter most welcome. It was a most striking exhibition of the division made by civil strife. On one thing we all agreed—we were to meet foemen worthy of our steel. The conspicuous service of Colonel Kenly in the war with Mexico, where, side by side with Watson, he so gallantly fought in the streets of Monterey, swept by the leaden hail of its defenders, had won for him the respect of every Marylander and made his reputation a part of the State's history. With several of his officers I had been on most friendly terms, until current events so widely separated us.

The attack was made with vigor, and Wheat's Louisiana Tigers, about 150 strong, were ordered to co-operate with us. Colonel Kenly withdrew rapidly from the town and took position on an elevation some half mile to the north. With a detachment of my company I was ordered to the skirmish line, which, under Lieutenant-Colonel Dorsey, at once engaged the enemy. Together with the Louisianians we held the enemy, closely pushing them on their right, while Colonel Johnson, with the remainder of the regiment, attacked their left with such success that they were forced to retire and cross the river, continuing their retreat in the direction of Middletown. Near Nineveh church, within a few miles, they were overtaken by our cavalry, which had come up in the meantime. The cavalry, although very much inferior in numbers, without hesitation attacked the retreating column. Colonel Kenly halted and made a stout resistance, but our men rode over him in a wild charge, which broke his command into a rout, in which the larger portion were captured, including Colonel Kenly, after receiving several wounds.

Whilst we were skirmishing, and just before Kenly began to retire, his cavalry, about two squadrons, as near as I can remember, came dashing forward as if they proposed to pick up my skirmishers, and when I found they were getting uncomfortably close, I rallied to the shelter of a stone fence and gave them such a reception as to send them galloping back in a hurry; but I more particularly remember the anxious entreaty of quite an elderly member of my company, who, as he saw the federal horse coming up in dangerous nearness, his faith in his young Lieutenant was somewhat shaken, and he said, "For God's sake, Lieutenant, don't let them pick us up!" As we sent them reeling back, I think he became reassured, for he followed me without question, not only that day, but afterward, until death claimed him about a month later in the action near Harrisonburg.

We were gathered around fires, engaged in making coffee, when the cavalry came in with their prisoners. Then ensued a strange scene, as the antagonists of a few hours back now freely mingled, acquaintances were renewed and enquiries made for absent ones. The next morning Colonel Johnson assembled all the officers who could be spared, and in a body went to the town and made formal call on Colonel Kenly and his officers, who were confined in the hospital building. Colonel Kenly was badly hurt and a number of his officers were seriously wounded and showed evidence of their rough handling. He seemed to be very much depressed at his misfortune and rather sullen in his demeanor toward us. In fact, when we retired it was with the conviction that our motives were not appreciated and our mission was a failure.

Jackson at once addressed himself to Banks, who was at Strasburg, and moved his own division in the direction of Middletown, on the Valley turnpike, between Strasburg and Winchester, pushing Ewell's division forward toward Winchester. This caused Banks to withdraw from Strasburg in considerable disorder, with the loss of material. He halted at Winchester and made preparation to give battle. The attack was made early on the 25th, and resulted in the utter defeat of Banks, who did not stop in his retreat until he crossed the river at Williamsport. Our regiment had been pushed forward in the early dawn, before it was sufficiently light enough to determine the position of the enemy. A very considerable fog prevailed, and we were soon shut off from sight of our own troops. We, therefore, halted, with our line resting on an apple orchard and in close proximity to some farm buildings.

It was evident the enemy was very near us, for we could hear them talking. In a little while a most terrific fire came from our right rear, and we afterwards learned that the 21st North Carolina, in their advance, had struck the federal line, which was posted behind a stone fence. The 21st was driven back with loss. Our situation was precarious; we were alone; no support was to be seen, and as far as we could determine we had interjected ourselves into the enemy's line. The only thing to do was to keep quiet until our troops moved forward and then join in the attack. This soon happened, and the fog lifting at the time, we saw our lines coming over the hills to the west of the town and Ewell advancing from our right and rear. Jackson, with his division and the brigade of Taylor, gallantly charged, and the federals, after some resistance, finding Ewell's movement threatened their line of retreat, gave way in disorder, when it became a race who should enter the town first. As we had the advantage from our advanced position, we reached the head of Main street as Taylor's Louisianians struck the western suburbs. As we came down the street at a double quick, the women came out of the houses and encouraged us with their smiles and greetings. They were wild with enthusiasm, and not a few threw their arms around some rugged, dirty soldier and kissed him.

For several months Winchester had been in the hands of the enemy, and the indignities they had suffered now rose up and made them almost frantic at the assurance of relief. Their sorrowful ministrations to our unfortunate wounded after Kernstown, were now turned to joy as they beheld the invaders in flight through their town, pursued closely by the confederate columns. It was a great time, and it was not to be wondered that some of our people lost their heads in the excitement. Lieutenant-Colonel Dorsey was one of these, for, leaving the main body, he rode down a side street and encountered a party of the retreating federals, who fired upon and badly wounded him. This closed his service with the regiment and, I believe, his career as a soldier as well, for, on recovery, the regiment had been disbanded and he entered the railroad service, where he was efficient during the remainder of the war.

We bivouacked that night some miles beyond Winchester. The results of these operations were some 3000 prisoners, two pieces of artillery and 10,000 small arms, besides stores in good quantities. The prisoners were sent to Richmond, with the exception of some few who were recaptured at Front Royal on the advance of Shields. The arms were secured, and the Quartermaster and Commissaries were busily engaged in securing the captured stores for the next few days, while the troops were given a day of rest. Among the strange things that had fallen into our hands were a number of sets of armor, metal breastplates and thigh protectors, which were found on the prisoners or in baggage of their camps. We amused ourselves by setting up these armor plates and firing at them at short range to test their power of resistance. At fair range they would turn a revolver ball very well, and a rifle or musket ball if from any considerable distance, but at close range they were vulnerable to the latter. It has been denied that these doughty warriors wore these appliances, but I can testify to their existence and use, and, moreover, Colonel Johnson succeeded in sending one to the rear and it is in his possession at the present writing.

The next day we moved to Martinsburg. Captain —— and myself obtained permission to go into the town, where we met Major Harding, our Quartermaster, who was in charge of the abandoned property of the enemy. The Major informed us that among other things confided to his tender mercy was the Adams Express Office, and invited us to enter and enjoy what we could find. This was an opportunity that seldom came to a hungry confederate, and we entered upon our investigations with most commendable promptness. The thoroughness of our search soon developed a prize, "a basket of champagne." The discovery called for a consultation at once. Here was a condition to which we had for a long time been strangers, and strategy was called into play to permit proper disposition of our "find" and to meet such an unlooked-for emergency in a becoming, dignified and soldierly manner. Our council of war was unanimous in its judgment that the dangerous property must be secured and not allowed to fall into hands where it might exercise its mischievous powers; therefore, we at once secured as much of the contents as we could conveniently carry on our persons, confiding the rest to discreet friends, and, suspending all further investigations as to other express matter in the office, we sought some secure place where, free from interruption, we could address ourselves to the mighty task in hand.

A room was secured in the hotel—I think it was the hotel, although my recollections are not very exact as to the details or minutiae of our operations. I can recall, however, that some hours later, or about midnight, —— waked me up and proposed we return to camp, where, in accordance with our terms of leave, we should have reported at sunset. Colonel Johnson and myself were at this time sharing blankets, and it was not only the proper thing that we should report our arrival to the commanding officer, but it was to a degree necessary for me to disturb him in order to get my share of cover. As a peace-offering I tendered him a lemon and a cake of toilet soap; the wine had been disposed of effectively. The

Colonel's good nature and the ludicrousness of the situation got the better of his indignation at our grievous infraction of discipline, and he bade me turn in and go to sleep. By day, as reveille sounded, the order to resume march was received, and we moved in the direction of Harper's Ferry, not halting until the vicinity of Halltown was reached. I have not forgotten the terrors of that day's march, particularly in the early hours, until some friend gave me a bottle of Rhine wine. To this day I have a most profound respect for Rhine wine; its vivifying influence made it to me the sweetest of all elixirs. It healed my sorrows, bound my wounds and enabled me to make the march with comparative comfort. Many years have since rolled by, many varied experiences have I undergone, but never since have I attempted to put away six bottles of champagne, single-handed, at one sitting.

The movement towards Harper's Ferry was followed by a demonstration against that post, but the stirring events which were happening in our rear summoned General Jackson to give attention to his lines of communication. His brilliant attack on Banks had occasioned the interruption of McDowell's march with 40,000 troops to unite with McClellan, who then had his lines in sight of the spires of Richmond, and with 20,000 men he started toward the Valley, making for Front Royal. Fremont, with 20,000 more, was beyond the North Mountain range, in the vicinity of the South Branch Valley, and, having gathered the discomfited forces of Milroy, was considering what next to do, when he was urgently directed from Washington to cross over into the main Valley and take position, say at Harrisonburg. After repeated orders, he finally moved and approached Strasburg from the direction of Wardensville. The situation for Jackson was critical. The concentration of these two forces, each of them largely outnumbering his own, at a point on his direct line of communication, cumbered as he was by prisoners, captured stores and material, required the promptest action to secure safety. General Winder, with his brigade, one regiment of which was then on Loudoun Heights, and the 1st

Maryland regiment, was left to bring up the rear, with orders to follow as soon as the 2d Virginia could be withdrawn, and coupled with the comforting assurance that Strasburg would be held until we could come up, but we must get there that night if possible. Strasburg was over forty miles away. It was nearly, if not quite, 9 A. M. when, on the arrival of the 2d Virginia, we were able to take up the march. Fortunately for us, although there was a large federal force in Harper's Ferry under General Saxton, we were not harassed or followed to any disagreeable extent. As for Banks and his army, it was over two weeks before he could be persuaded to recross the river and move toward Winchester. All the day we marched steadily, halting only for a few moments at a time as a breathing spell. The roads were quite muddy and the passage of the trains and troops with Jackson had made them not the best for marching purposes. There was no straggling, for all knew the penalty of dropping out or falling behind the column would be capture by the enemy.

Those who for physical causes had to succumb were placed in wagons or ambulances, and but very few were left behind or captured. It was an emergency that called for the exercise of all the endurance at our command. In the early shades of night we reached Winchester, but still the march kept on. Strasburg was still twenty miles away. By midnight we had reached Newtown, when flesh and blood could no longer respond to the relentless demand to keep on, and as we heard that Jackson was yet at Strasburg, holding that point, a halt of a couple of hours was made, and down in the road we dropped and slept. The approach of early dawn called us up again, and the sound of the guns in the direction of Strasburg quickened our tired steps as we resumed the march. As we approached Middletown we had intelligence that McDowell's column had reached Front Royal, and the advance under Shields was but a few miles from our flank and would soon reach the turnpike on which we were marching. The phase of this new danger called for renewed effort, and by noon we were in sight of Strasburg and could see Jackson's lines as he stood confronting Fremont and holding open for us the road. The batteries on either side were actively engaged, but Fremont was unwilling to attack, and under the cover of our lines we passed through the town and stopped only when we had reached Fisher's Hill, safe in the fold.

Surely, we thought, a night's rest would be given us at this point, but in a little while our lines were withdrawn and the march resumed and halt not made until after dark in the vicinity of Maurertown. These additional miles were made under the helpful influence of "grog." One of our regimental wagons became stuck in a small stream crossing the turnpike near Cedar Creek and was abandoned. Several of our men who had fallen out that morning, and who were evidently foraging for something to eat, came along after the command had passed, leaving the wagon to its fate, but these boys went to a neighboring house, found a pair of horses, impressed them and unloaded the wagon of its entire contents save one single barrel, and that of whiskey, and succeeded in extricating the wagon, and as we were lying on the roadside at Fisher's Hill, to our great surprise, came thundering up the road, when Bush, the driver, reported his rescue of the wagon, with the loss of all the "superfluities," as he termed the original contents, except the barrel of whiskey. To roll out the barrel, knock out the head, was but the work of a moment, and as the regiment formed again to take up the march, a liberal draught was given to each man, and more miles made under circumstances seemingly impossible. The next few days were days of trial. The pursuit from Strasburg was close, and frequently our cavalry was driven in on our rear, necessitating a halt and forming a line of battle to repel the pursuers. To fall out of line for ten minutes meant capture. The head of the enemy's column was nearly always in sight, and when night came on strong guards were posted to repel night attacks.

This condition existed until we reached Harrisonburg, when the long marches of the enemy and the fatigued condition of their men gave us a little more time to take a comfortable long breath and rest.

The heavy rains of the preceding few days had deluged the country and caused the Shenandoah to rise to an unfordable degree. The bridge at Mount Crawford having been destroyed, our march in the direction of Staunton was rendered impracticable. Shields, with his command, had advanced up the Luray Valley on the eastern side of the river at the same time Fremont was so relentlessly pressing us up the main Valley. The bridge at Port Republic, some nine miles to the eastward of Harrisonburg, was still intact, and Jackson determined to move in that direction and, if possible, strike Shields before he could form a junction with Fremont. On June 6th we moved from Harrisonburg on the Port Republic road. As soon as we left the turnpike our troubles began, and during the day we did not progress more than three or four miles, owing to the soft condition of the roads, which became quagmires as soon as the trains moved over them, forcing us to take the fields, which were but little better. The army was literally floundering in the mud, and the persistency of the enemy, who closely followed us, made our rear a post of miserable discomfort. Bayard, who was leading Fremont's advance, with the 1st New Jersey Cavalry, under Col. Sir Percy Wyndham, and the Pennsylvania Rifles or Bucktails, under Colonel Kane, was hammering away at our rear guard, which could not move because of the stalled condition of our trains. He evidently thought that Jackson was now caught in his own trap, but discretion was sacrificed to valor when he ventured to attack Ashby, who turned upon him in a successful charge, in which Wyndham and some fifty or sixty of his men were made prisoners. To retrieve this disaster, Bayard pushed his infantry to the front, when Ashby reported to General Ewell that it would be necessary to support him with infantry and check the troublesome foe, who were endangering the safety of our trains. We had reached a point some four or four and one-half miles from Harrisonburg, and the afternoon was well spent, when General Ewell directed our regiment and the 58th Virginia to retrace our steps and assist General Ashby. We had gone but a short distance when we were turned into a heavy body of oak wood and formed in line of battle. General Ashby reported the enemy were in position at the farther end of the timber, and gave it as his judgment they were but dismounted cavalry, and if we would move forward promptly we would be able to "take them in," as he expressed himself. Captain Nicholas and myself were detached, with a portion of our respective companies, and directed to deploy as skirmishers and advance until we developed the enemy. We had not moved forward but a few hundred yards before we found the object of our search, and, under the cover of the woods, I succeeded in getting down pretty close to their line, when, to my surprise, instead of cavalry I discovered a well-formed infantry line, sheltered behind a stout fence on the edge of the timber. Halting my line, I made my way back and so reported. Generals Ewell and Ashby were together, but the latter insisted I was mistaken. The 58th Virginia was directed to move forward to the point where my line was formed, when I was to advance and fire signal shots, and then they were to charge the enemy. It was a well laid plan, but it failed most woefully in execution. I returned to my skirmishers, Nicholas being somewhat to the right, moved my line forward and fired the signal shots, when the 58th, with a loud cheer, advanced, to be met with a staggering fire from the Bucktails, who poured volley after volley into us as our line hesitated and finally halted and began to return the fire. My position was decidedly uncomfortable; we were between the two lines and subjected to the fire from both. Fortunately for us, the 58th, in their confusion, were firing too high to do execution. If the Bucktails had been in the tree tops, I think it likely they mostly would have been killed. As it was, they remained on *terra firma*, and with great coolness and deliberation kept up a most effective fire. For some ten minutes or more it appeared almost certain we would be wiped out. The 58th was of good material. Their subsequent record fully redeemed their misbehavior on this day, but they were most horribly and inefficiently commanded. Taking private Ackler, of my company, I carried their colors forward and implored them to stop firing and charge with us, but they were immovable, and Ackler was shot down by my side. At this juncture General Ashby rode forward and urged them to advance, riding through their line, begging them to rally and follow him, but without avail. He then commenced firing his pistol at the federal line, which was such a short distance off. Under the withering fire of the enemy he soon fell, and the gallant soldier was no more.

I had just determined to make an effort to extricate my men, when, with a familiar yell, our regiment, under Colonel Johnson, came charging forward on the flank of the enemy and broke their line, and as they retired over the open field, Nicholas moved down with his end of the skirmish line, and under the combined destructive fire the Bucktails fell as thick as leaves in Vallombrosa. Colonel Kane was left on the field badly wounded and fell into our hands. It was impossible to pursue the advantage, as the federal batteries and supports covered the field in our front, and it was not the intention to bring on a general engagement.

The loss of the regiment in this affair was quite heavy. Captain Robertson, of I company, was killed, also my dear friend, Lieutenant Snowden, and private Beatty, of my own company. The 58th Virginia also suffered severely and paid penalty for their indecision, while the death of Ashby was a misfortune which could not be repaired. Take the affair altogether, it was a sad incident, the only redeeming feature of which was the gallant example set by Colonel Johnson and his command, which was duly recognized by General Ewell in general orders authorizing the regiment to append to their color staff, as a trophy, one of the captured bucktails, the insignia of the command which so bravely and at such cost resisted our attack.

In the shades of the evening we gathered our dead and wounded and took up the march a mile or two further on, when we halted for the night. Early the next morning we buried our dead comrades and then took position at Cross-Keys, where Fremont attacked in force and was successfully repulsed by General Ewell with his division, Jackson having moved with his own division to Port Republic, to protect the bridge and check the advance of Shields.

On June 9th Jackson crossed the bridge at Port Republic with his division and moved to attack the advance of Shields, which had taken position about a mile and one-half north of the town, withdrawing the brigades of Elzey and Taylor in support and leaving that noble old soldier, General Trimble, with his brigade, to confront Fremont's entire force and to cover the movement, with instructions to follow. Shields's command was made up of sterner material than our antagonists at Cross-Keys, and in the early part of the action handled Jackson's advanced brigades very roughly, until Taylor, with his Louisianians, took them in flank, capturing their battery and causing the retirement of their lines, which, under the renewed attack, gave way and retreated, losing heavily in prisoners, together with six pieces of artillery. We reached the field at the close of the action; all about us were the evidences of the stout resistance, and while we were engaged caring for the wounded friends and foes, the lines of Fremont emerged on the hills bordering the western side of the river, and their guns soon opened fire upon our people in the meadows where the battle had been fought, forcing us to forego our merciful ministrations and to retire out of range of their artillery.

The destruction of the bridge at Port Republic by Jackson, as he withdrew to the eastern side of the river, prevented any further advance by Fremont, and as soon as he ascertained the defeat and rout of Shields, considerations for his own safety led him to return to Harrisonburg and in a few days to Strasburg. In the meantime McDowell summoned Shields to recross the mountain and rejoin him in his march to the relief of McClellan. This terminated the memorable Valley campaign of Jackson. Within the short period of sixty days he had defeated four armies, captured eight pieces of artillery, 4000 prisoners and vast quantities of army stores, wagons, etc. In addition to this, he had completely disarranged the federal plan of campaign; diverted troops intended for union with McClellan's right wing before

Richmond, to the defense of Washington; created a panic which paralyzed the federal movements and opened the way for Lee's attack, which resulted in the raising of the siege of Richmond, and hurried McClellan to the protection of his gunboats on the lower James. The arduous marches and losses incident to such a severe service depleted our ranks, however. Ewell's division scarcely numbered one-half the strength it had when it left the Rappahannock in March.

With Port Republic virtually ended my service on foot, as at the earnest request of Colonel Johnson I again assumed the duties of regimental Adjutant, and so continued until the regiment was mustered out of service in August.

From Port Republic we were sent to Staunton to rest and recruit. In a few days, however, troops arrived from Richmond, the brigades of Whiting and Lawton, and we all looked forward to a return to the lower Valley; but, much to our surprise, were placed on the cars and moved through Charlottesville and Gordonsville to Frederick's Hall, from which point we marched to Ashland, where we arrived on June 25th. It was now evident that Jackson was about to take part in the relief of Richmond. The next day the march was resumed in the direction of Pole Green church, a short distance from McClellan's right wing at Mechanicsville. Our progress was somewhat slow, being impeded by the enemy's cavalry and the obstructed condition of the roads from felled trees and destroyed bridges, through which means the enemy hoped to delay our march. They were so successful in this that toward evening, when the heavy firing near Mechanicsville indicated that our troops had crossed the Chickahominy and were attacking the enemy in their intrenched lines, we were some miles from our designated position. Hill's attack of Ellyson's Mill was repulsed with great loss, but our combined movement forced Porter to withdraw to Gaines Mill or Cold Harbor in the night.

On the morning of the 27th the confederate attack was renewed and a most severe battle raged, with varying fortune, until toward sunset the confederate line swept the field and the defeated enemy withdrew to the north side of the Chickahominy, leaving in our hands guns, prisoners and their dead and wounded in large numbers. Our own loss was extremely heavy, but, fortunately, that of our regiment was comparatively light. General Jackson had placed us early in the afternoon in support of his reserve artillery, and from our position directed the movements of his command. The musketry was terrible, and it would roll toward us as the federals advanced their line and then recede, as our brave men would hurl themselves upon them and drive them back. These fluctuations of sound would indicate to us the progress being made, and as we could not see very much from our position, several times during the afternoon Lieut. Frank Bond and myself would mount our horses and ride forward to where we could see our lines and then return with report of what we had observed. We saw Elzey take his brigade into action, entering the wood which the federal line occupied, and from which he was soon brought badly wounded. Then were borne back the dead bodies of the brave Wheat of the Tigers, McDonald of the staff and Colonel Allen of the 2d Virginia, but the old brigade held on to its work and steadily pressed forward. Not only in our front was this terrible fire maintained, but all along our lines to our right did the same condition prevail. The rebel yell was mingled with the federal shout. At one time it appeared that no substantial progress was being made, and the sun was going down as if weary of the bloody strife. General Jackson was evidently disturbed; his usual quiet and cool manner now evidenced restlessness and anxiety. He would ride up and down the road, listening intently, receiving reports and sending out his orders. Then he would stop and, raising his hand and bowing his head, appeal to his God in the fervency of prayer. From one of these moments of solemn silence he seemed to gather himself together, somewhat nervously, and, riding quickly to where Colonel Johnson was sitting on his horse, exclaimed: "Colonel, take your regiment in." Our moment had evidently come. "In which direction shall I go, General?" replied Johnson. "Over there, sir, over there," was the reply, indicating by a movement of his hand a quarter in which the din of the firing had broken out with renewed violence. In a moment the regiment was advancing, and as we struck the edge of the woods the ground sloped in our front toward a swamp, through which it was impossible to ride. Colonel Johnson, Lieutenant Bond, Drs. Johnson and Latimer, our surgeons, and myself, the mounted officers, had to dismount, and with the men pushed or waded through the swamp as best we could to the other side. Once over, the line reformed, we advanced to the crest of the high ground, and before us was the open plateau on which the battle was raging. Marching over a line of men who were lying down awaiting orders, we moved forward across the open field and were at once under heavy fire. Before us were several regiments of our troops coming back in some disorder; these we halted and encouraged to face about and unite with us in our advance. They were North Carolina troops and, to their credit be it said, many of them rallied and formed on our line. The fire of the enemy now grew very heavy. Colonel Johnson halted for a moment, had the regiment to dress on the colors and then put them through the manual of arms. This steadied our line, and the command, "Forward!" was again given. Then came riding toward us from our right a mounted officer, who proved to be Lieut. McHenry Howard, of General Winder's staff and a former member of the regiment, with a message from the General, that if we could halt a few moments he would unite with his brigade in the attack. This was done, and with a yell we started our final charge. The enemy in our immediate front proved to be regular troops, under the command of General Sykes, an officer of distinction. Their position was strengthened by being in somewhat of a sunken road, which gave to them the advantage of protection and cover. It so happened that this movement was made at the time of the general advance all along our lines, and in the coming twilight—for it was approaching night—the furious assault was successful and the federal lines gave way. In our advance we struck the McGhee house and a cluster of farm buildings, which caused our lines to break until the obstruction was passed. But our men did not falter, but rapidly reformed and pressed forward. At this point we took a number of prisoners and secured some horses. General Reynolds had his headquarters here. I fortunately secured one of the horses, a stout sorrel, which gave me a mount and did me good service until used up in the Maryland campaign. After passing the McGhee house we captured two guns which the enemy left in their flight, and as it was now quite dark the line was halted and the pursuit called off. A most tremendous cheering at this time from the direction of the enemy, gave rise to some apprehension on our part that our lines to the right had not been so successful, but in a little while we knew that the enemy had been driven entirely from the field. From what I have sinced learned, this cheering was from troops who had crossed the river to Porter's support and under whose protection he was making his way to the other side.

Just before we reached the McGhee house, Lieutenant Bond and myself, being in company, agreed we should look after each other. In the confusion of passing the obstructions we became separated, and as the advance was resumed I missed him and at once concluded he had fallen, so started back to look him up. I found him at the McGhee buildings, however, very actively engaged in getting some horses out of the stable, and it was here I got my sorrel cob.

We spent the night in this position. Coffee was in supply, as our federal prisoners were plentifully supplied, and we did not hesitate to ask a share, while the contents of the haversacks of the dead and wounded offered additional means of meeting our wants.

One very singular incident at this point was the finding of General Lee's order detailing the entire movement for the attack on McClellan. At this time the organization of the army was in divisions, and the order set forth the instructions to each Division commander, from the crossing at Mechanicsville and on. This particular order found at the McGhee house was addressed to Gen. D. H. Hill. How it came there in the enemy's line, Heaven only knows, but it is a fact that one of our men found it, carried it to Colonel Johnson and he permitted me to read it that night. I remember distinctly that in reading the order I was impressed with the fidelity with which, to that time, the instructions had been carried out, and recalled the celebrated order of General Scott for one of his battles in the Valley of Mexico, which has been so frequently quoted as an evidence of his far-seeing ability and of faithfulness on the part of his subordinates in execution. The circumstance of this lost order has not been made public to any extent, but not very long since General Johnson asked me if I remembered the event, the facts concerning which, I believe, were known but to him and myself. It is a singular coincidence that Lee's campaign in Maryland, in the following September, was exposed to McClellan by means of a similar lost general order, which set forth the operations of the army and its dispersion in the movement against Harper's Ferry. This lost order was also addressed to Gen. D. H. Hill, and was handed to McClellan as he approached Frederick, and at once gave him confidence to press forward and carry the mountain passes at South Mountain and Crampton's Gap, knowing how feebly they were held and that Lee's army was scattered from Harper's Ferry to Hagerstown. It has been pretty clearly shown, however, that this last-named order, although intended for General Hill, was never in his possession, having either been lost by the courier, or, as has been claimed, the courier was wounded and the order taken from him. The misfortune, however it occurred, is responsible for the weakened and illy-prepared condition in which the Army of Northern Virginia received McClellan's attack at Sharpsburg. It is more than probable that but for the order getting into the enemy's hands he would have moved so slowly as to have permitted Lee to concentrate and fight elsewhere.

The next morning, June 28th, the confederate columns resumed their advance, and it was soon apparent that McClellan had determined to abandon his Richmond lines and retire, but whether down the peninsula or in the direction of the James river was not so well defined. Valuable time was lost and very heavy fighting took place before it was fully developed that the protection of his gunboats on the James was the haven in which he sought to shelter his disappointed and depleted forces. To aid in the solution of this problem, General Ewell was directed, with his division, in which was the 1st Maryland, to move to Dispatch Station, on the Richmond & York River Railroad. Our occupancy of this point demonstrated that McClellan had abandoned his White House line, and the destruction of vast supplies of stores and material indicated the haste and pressure under which his withdrawal was being made. Dispatch Station was just south of the Chickahominy. The only force of the enemy we found at this point was a body of cavalry, which retired on our advance. In the meantime the federals had set fire to the railroad bridge and then started a train, loaded with ammunition, in our direction. Fire was applied to the train, which came thundering down the road, threatening to cross the bridge and plunge into our midst, a number of our men being engaged at the time in destroying the railroad. As the train entered upon the bridge, however, a mighty explosion occurred, making a most fearful report and one of the most magnificent sights it was ever my fortune to witness. The volumes of smoke rose in the most ponderous clouds, which assumed the grandest proportions, attracting the interest of all who beheld. We held our breath in admiration of the scene, forgetting all sense of danger as the clouds rose toward the heavens in such varied and fantastical shapes. This episode assured General Ewell that the enemy was either making for the Williamsburg road or the James, and he at once formed his division and marched toward White Oak Swamp, where Jackson was in position.

The next morning, June 30th, it was confidently expected Jackson would force the passage over the swamp and interrupt the line of the federal retreat, which followed a road on the highlands on the other side and in view of our position. I believe it is generally conceded that the failure to make this movement was the only serious mistake ever attributed to this great soldier. It has been explained on the ground of his exhaustion. The demands that had been made upon his physical endurance had been honored, until nature gave way and refused to respond any further to the insatiable exigencies of the occasion. It was so foreign to his character to let go such a golden opportunity, that no other plausible reason can be assigned for his inactivity during these important hours. It certainly was not in accord with his nature or instincts as a soldier to lie dormant while Longstreet was fighting at Frazier's farm or Glendale. It has been suggested that Jackson believed his men had performed their share of fighting, and out of regard for them he held back. This idea is so far from his usual course as not to be tolerated for a moment. He was naturally so combative and earnest in his work that whenever brought into contact with the enemy his first and only promptings were to strike the blow. If, as usual, he had met with success, and his men were worn out and tired, he reasoned, in how much worse condition must be his antagonist who had been discomfited. No; there is no rational explanation of his failure to attack at this momentous juncture but the theory of his utter physical prostration, and when is recalled the character of the enormous strain, physical and mental, to which he had been subjected for the sixty days previous, it can be readily understood how affronted nature sullenly refused to respond to additional effort.

The consequences were, however, far-reaching. The bloody repulse at Malvern might have been obviated and the federal retreat seriously jeopardized, had fate ordered otherwise. As it was, McClellan succeeded in reaching the Malvern position in fair shape, although his losses in battle were heavy. The position taken by McClellan at Malvern was one of great natural strength. It was not unduly extended, and with his still ample force he was enabled to form heavy lines of defense, while the ground was particularly adapted to the efficient handling of his artillery, in which arm he was so superior to Lee in guns and in their character. From the confederate side the ground offered but little opportunity to use artillery. In addition to these advantages, the federal gunboats in the river gave comfort and material assistance.

When General Lee became convinced that McClellan's objective was the James, he ordered the occupation of Malvern Hill, but the officer to whom the movement was confided failed to realize the importance of prompt and decisive action and permitted the federal advance to divert him from the execution of the important operation. Had Malvern been occupied as General Lee desired, McClellan would have been forced to continue his march to the lower river, and with the unremitting pursuit which would have followed it is more than probable that he would have been destroyed in the attempt to escape.

On July 1st battle was joined at Malvern. The confederate attack was as heroic as the federal defense was stern and abiding. To sum up the day's work, it was a decided repulse for us, and while the enemy did not assume the offensive, yet we made no considerable impression on their lines. Night came on—a night of horror that will never be forgotten. The wounded of both armies lay mingled on the field, each line holding its original position. Their cries for water and for help were most piteous, and yet little could be done to alleviate their suffering. The 1st Maryland had been held by General Jackson until late in the evening, and then we were ordered in to hold and picket the front of his command. We halted amid the dead and dying. During the night, as I made up the relief details for picket duty, more than once an attempt was made to arouse a dead man. Just before midnight a courier rode up enquiring for General Jackson, and, as we could not direct him to headquarters, he said he bore a message from General Lee, to be delivered to any officer of rank on the field, if General Jackson could not be reached. The purport of this message was that if the enemy advanced in the morning, in view of the heavy loss of the day and the disorganized condition of our troops, it would be necessary to retire toward the Richmond lines, and General Jackson would be expected to cover such withdrawal. It was, therefore, with anxious hearts we waited for the coming dawn. At last the night of horrors wore away and the faint light in the east gave promise of the coming day. Just as it became light enough to see, we discovered in our front what looked to be a heavy body of cavalry moving steadily across the field. The firing of our outposts soon gave assurance of their character, and we naturally concluded what General Lee apprehended was now to be made manifest. Colonel Johnson at once formed the regiment and sent me to notify the troops on our left to be prepared for the enemy's advance. These troops I found to be Georgians, under General Lawton, who roused his men and made proper disposition for the threatened attack. To our great relief, however, the federal column continued their movement across our front and then disappeared toward our left, and our pickets were pushed forward, only to find that McClellan had gone. To say this was a relief would be to feebly describe our feelings. We were painfully aware of the shattered condition of our troops, at least those where we were, but it appears the enemy had also suffered great loss and McClellan did not think it safe to remain, with the possibility of receiving a renewed attack the next day. To state it fairly, both sides were entirely satisfied to be relieved of the presence of the other.

The federals moved to a position lower down the river at Westover, where, under the protection of their fleet and intrenchments, which were promptly thrown up, they sought relief and rest from their troublesome adversaries.

The siege of Richmond was raised. The hosts that in view of its spires had for weeks boasted they would soon occupy the fair city were now themselves shut up in narrow confines, protected by the guns of their fleet, after having suffered a series of defeats, with the loss of millions in material, fifty-two pieces of artillery, with some 16,000 men killed, wounded and prisoners. The confederate loss was also heavy, as the federals occupied intrenched or strong positions and received the attack.

During the later hours of the afternoon at Malvern our regiment was posted in a body of oak timber, and General Jackson had his headquarters on the roadside immediately on our left. We were subjected to the fire of the gunboats in the river and from the enemy's batteries in our front.

Great trees were shattered as they were struck by shells from the heavy guns of the fleet, and the infernal explosion of these projectiles was a new experience to us. It was a positive relief to hear the shells from the field pieces; so marked was the difference between the two that it was more like the sound of a pop cracker as compared with that of a musket. We sought shelter behind the trees as best we could, but the falling branches and shattered tree tops were flying around us, and every now and then some noble oak would be splintered from trunk to top. Major Dabney, of General Jackson's staff, was a Presbyterian of the straightest Calvinistical sort, while Captain Nelson, his fellow staff officer, was an Episcopalian. Doubtless these gentlemen had frequently discussed their theological differences, and now when Captain Nelson saw the Major behind a sheltering oak the circumstance gave him an opportunity for practical argument which even the gravity and seriousness of the occasion did not suppress. "Come from behind that tree, Doctor; if it is ordained you are to be killed, the tree will not save you." The Doctor was unquestionably true to his convictions, but still was not unmindful of the sense of security which two feet of oak inspires, particularly when placed between one's weak body and the fearful missiles which were being hurled in our midst. During one of the short lulls in the firing, Colonel Johnson, Lieutenant Bond and myself mounted and rode down the road to the front. We had gone only a few hundred yards, when we noticed a number of men straggling, as we thought, through the woods on either side of the road, but paid no especial attention to them. A little further on the road made somewhat of a sharp turn to the left, at the same time ascended quite a hill, and as we reached the crest the ground in our front was an open field to the left, extending some distance to the front, while on our right was a house surrounded by a fence enclosing, perhaps, an acre of ground and the buildings. As we took this rapidly in our vision, another circumstance made a deeper impression and gave us the immediate conviction that it was a decidedly unhealthy location, for not more than 100 yards from where we were was a federal line of battle. It is curious, but it did not require a word to indicate what was passing through our respective minds, but our action was identical and absolutely in perfect accord one with the other. It did not require the persuasion of the bullets which came from the federal line to convince us we had made a mistake, nor did our natural obstinacy interfere with the prompt acknowledgment of our error, or our soldierly pride prevent a hasty retirement. We saw, we turned, we fled in much less time than that in which these lines are written. We had approached and reached the federal line unobserved. We immediately rode back, and Colonel Johnson reported to General Jackson where we had been and what we had observed and asked permission to take the regiment forward, claiming that if he could get them where we had been without detection, with a volley and a charge the federal line would be taken by surprise and their defeat easy. General Jackson said: "No; remain where you are." Perhaps he was right, for at dusk, when we did move up to this position, the ground was covered with our dead and wounded, there being not less than fifty in the small enclosure around the house previously mentioned.

The usual rains which attend and follow a great battle now set in, and throughout the day it poured in torrents, while the work of burying the dead, caring for the wounded and getting the various commands in shape was prosecuted.

The following day, July 3d, the advance was resumed, and on reaching the vicinity of Westover, where McClellan had taken refuge, the army was distributed so as to invest that position. Immediately on reaching the federal lines Jackson made dispositions for attack, which was suspended on the arrival of General Longstreet, who suggested that an examination of the enemy's position be made by General Whiting. This examination was not favorable to prospective success, and consequently we contented ourselves with active skirmishing with the enemy. General Early, who had been wounded at Williamsburg on the retirement from the peninsula in May, now joined us and took command of the brigade, General Elzey having been badly wounded at Gaines' Mill.

The enemy's position in our front was exceedingly strong naturally, and he had added to its security by throwing up intrenchments, cutting down trees and making obstructions, and by the concentration of his batteries commanded thoroughly the ground over which we would have to move to the attack. It is no reflection on the fortitude of our men to say they were immensely relieved by the restraining opinion of General Whiting. The overworked condition of their bodies and the severe strain to which their nervous systems had been subjected during the past week of incessant labor and bloodshed was now followed by a reaction, which made all satisfied to rest on the laurels which had been won. Even so gallant and distinguished a soldier as Gen. Charles S. Winder was led to intimate to General Jackson that his command was not "boiling over" for a resumption of hostilities. In this feeling, however, Jackson did not participate, and was rather indignant and severe in his rejoinder. If he had not been restrained by Longstreet, he would have assaulted the federal position as soon as his division could have been thrown forward on his arrival before Harrison's Landing. There is but little doubt, if the pursuit had been close and persistent, the federals could have been prevented from occupying the strong position they now held, and the demoralized condition they were in when they reached the river, approaching almost to disorganization, from their own accounts, under a bold and well-organized attack, would have settled the fate of the Army of the Potomac; but the day after Malvern found us in such sad plight that no movement, save that of Stuart with the cavalry was made, and when on the succeeding day the army reached the federal lines, the enemy had recovered from disorder to a degree, and the positions commanding the river flats, where they were massed, were strongly occupied and rendered secure from attack.

General Lee, therefore, in a few days determined, from sanitary as well as military reasons, to withdraw his army to the Richmond lines, leaving the cavalry to observe McClelian. This officer was not disposed, however, to move out to any distance, as he was contented and thankful for his escape and well occupied with the task of reorganizing his army and repairing the damage he had sustained.

For a week or so the 1st Maryland was camped within a few miles of Richmond, on the line of the Virginia Central Railroad. While here I made several visits into the city, which had been converted into a huge hospital. The unbounded hospitality of its citizens led them to open their homes to the sick and wounded soldier, and the women were lavish in their attention to the wants of the unfortunate. Full of joy and gratitude that the invader had been driven from their gates, there were few households but were touched by some sorrow in the death or disablement of some loved one. Their very griefs, however, found relief in the tender and loving ministrations which they bestowed on the poor soldiers who had suffered in their defense. The greater the stranger the greater the sympathy and kindness bestowed. This characteristic of these noble people all through the struggle of four long, weary years, even when dire poverty and distress was the lot of the former affluent, and had but lessened the character of service they were now able to render, created all over the southland an affection which will abide as long as the memories of their heroic sacrifice and devotion live in the hearts of a grateful people. To the confederate soldier of the Army of Northern Virginia, Richmond will be ever the Mecca enshrined in his heart.

About the middle of July Colonel Johnson was directed to proceed with the regiment to Charlottesville and to make effort to recruit its depleted ranks. The reputation it had won throughout the army, and the many Marylanders who were at this time crossing the Potomac into Virginia, led us to hope the losses of the campaign would be recovered and our ranks filled to an effective command. At Charlottesville we spent nearly a month—the most delightful month of our army experience. We had plenty to eat; the duties were limited to the ordinary routine of camp guard and police, while in the delightful society of the fair girls and the hospitable people of the town and neighborhood we found a pleasure to which we had long been strangers. Our younger people all went a-courting, and even some of the older and married sort were somewhat inclined to conceal the fact that they were Benedicts. Picnics at Monticello, dances and concerts and flirting with the girls occupied the full time at our disposal. To our sorrow, however, we did not succeed materially in recruiting the command. The general desire of those just coming over appeared to be to form new organizations, and the thirst for position on the part of certain prominent Marylanders who were in Richmond, but not in the army, fostered not only this desire, but soon bore evidences in the return of the dissatisfaction which pervaded and so nearly wrecked the regiment in May. There was a growing conviction among the men that injustice had been shown them in their enlistment. When the companies which enlisted for "three years or the war" found other companies mustered out at the expiration of one year, those who were held resented very strongly the distinction that had been made. The men, with very few exceptions, were not prompted by a purpose to leave the service—to their credit be it recorded, that generally, in fact almost universally, they re-entered the army—but they were anxious, many of them, to try other branches or arms of the service. In the idleness of these summer days this leaven of unrighteousness began to work, and even some of the officers did not oppose, if they did not actually encourage, the malcontents. A committee of the men came to me and solicited my co-operation. They held to me this alluring temptation, that their purpose was to reinlist and form a new regiment of which I was to be made Major. I am glad to this day that I had the common sense and appreciation of duty to refuse to be so influenced, and that I can truthfully say that by no assistance of mine, in word, thought or deed, was the dissolution of the 1st Maryland Infantry accomplished; and it is a further cause of thankfulness that I was not present at that sorrowful scene when Colonel Johnson had read the order of the War Department mustering it out of service. The order came without warning, and while it pleased the dissatisfied, it was received with indignation by the larger number of the men, who were attached to their officers and proud of the reputation the regiment had achieved. I had been sent to Lynchburg in charge of a large number of prisoners, and on my return to Charlottesville met Colonel Johnson, who told me he had mustered out the regiment the previous day, August 17th, 1862, near Gordonsville, and that we were now "free lances" and without commissions.

In closing the record of the 1st Maryland Infantry something should be said of the character of its *personnel*. It was made up of the very best material of the State. All classes and conditions found representation in its rank and file, from the proudest families to the humblest mechanic. It was, when in its prime, the largest Maryland command ever organized in the confederate service. It gave to the army one Major-General and two Brigadiers, while from its ranks went forward scores who prominently filled other positions in the line and in the staff. Nearly every family of prominence in the State was represented in its membership, and it proudly asserted its claim as the true successors of the Maryland Line of Continental fame. It wrote its right to that claim on the battlefield and in the official reports of the officers under whom it served. Its history should be familiar to all Marylanders through all time, and its fame the proud heritage of our loved Commonwealth, while should be reprobated those who were instrumental in destroying one of the finest commands in the confederate service.

The successive defeat of Milroy, of Banks, of Fremont and of Shields by Jackson led to the consolidation of their commands and the formation of a large army for the defense of Washington, to the command of which was assigned an officer who had risen to prominence in the western army, Maj.-Gen. John Pope. This hero came with his fame proudly sounded. He had been accustomed to see the backs of his enemies. He had no use for lines of retreat. The front was the place of honor and glory. Shame and disaster lurked in the rear, and it was further announced that under his victorious leadership headquarters would be in the saddle. The Army of Virginia, as his legions were denominated, some 40,000 strong, to be reinforced by the corps of Burnside, which had been withdrawn from North Carolina and sent to Fredericksburg for that purpose, had taken position in the county of Culpeper and threatened with its advance the post of Gordonsville, so important to us as a railway point. To meet this imminent danger, General Lee sent Jackson, with his own and Ewell's division, to Gordonsville in the latter part of July. In a few days the light division of A. P. Hill was ordered to join Jackson, it being manifest that nothing was to be apprehended in the way of renewal of the offensive by McClellan.

Jackson then determined to strike Pope's advance, under Banks, and on August 8th was fought the battle of Cedar Mountain, which resulted in Banks being driven from the field, with heavy loss, including one piece of artillery and some 5000 small arms. The confederate loss was also heavy for the force engaged—some 1200 men killed and wounded; included in the former was Brig.-Gen. Charles S. Winder, the commander of the "Stonewall Brigade." This distinguished Maryland soldier fell early in action. He was a most lovable character; quiet in his manner as a woman, his personal graces were only excelled by his military abilities. "None knew him but to love him, none named him but to praise." Maryland was represented in this action by the Maryland and Chesapeake batteries of artillery under Dement and Brown, and their gallant and efficient service is duly acknowledged in the official reports. Major Snowden Andrews, commanding a battalion of artillery, was severely wounded, and it was thought beyond doubt he would not survive his injuries, but, as General Early said, he had determined not to die, and "did live and recover in spite of the prediction of the doctors." This was Pope's first introduction to Jackson, and he had now an opportunity to view the faces of his enemy. The result of the action added to the uncomfortable feeling at Washington, and determined the immediate withdrawal of McClellan, particularly as General Lee was now moving with Longstreet to Jackson's support, with the purpose of overwhelming Pope before McClellan's troops could unite with him.

On the disbandment of the regiment on August 17th most of the officers and men went to Richmond. Colonel Johnson and myself remained at Charlottesville, until it became apparent that General Lee was about to move on Pope, when we joined the army, reporting to General Ewell, and, being without commissions or commands, we were merely lookers-on for a few days, and guests at headquarters, until the forward movement began. I learned after the war, I believe, that Colonel Johnson made effort at this time to have General Ewell appoint me to his staff, but without success, as Ewell thought I was too young for the responsibilities. Not being aware of the circumstance, I was spared the mortification of being turned down, and did not have the knowledge of my grievous disabilities to painfully restrain my ardor or flow of spirit. I am glad the fault was one which I overcame with time. It is more than possible that, under similar circumstances, I think, the objection would now be raised that I was too old. That condition unfortunately is beyond recovery. I bear no malice, however, against the old hero. He doubtless was quite right in his judgment.

The reputation which Colonel Johnson had achieved in command of the old regiment was appreciated by Generals Jackson and Ewell, and they were both anxious to have his services in a fitting command. The opportunity soon offered. One of the brigades of Jackson's division was without a commander of rank, General Jones being absent, sick, and the ranking officer was Major John Seddon, of the Irish Battalion. This officer was a brother of the Secretary of War and also a personal friend of Johnson's. He was a true gentleman, whose friendship, the result of coming association, I learned to prize most highly. On receiving an intimation from General Jackson that he would like to place Colonel Johnson in command, and the circumstances were fully explained that such action would be entirely without warrant from the standpoint of strict military construction, he generously waived his rights and with the greatest of courtesy and earnestness gave assurance of his entire satisfaction and approval of the proposed arrangement, promising his hearty co-operation and support. The order was then issued, and Colonel Johnson assumed command of the brigade before the crossing of the Rappahannock. The service of this brigade in the subsequent great engagements at Groveton or Second Manassas, General Jackson reported, in recommending Johnson for promotion, fully justified this rather irregular procedure. At Colonel Johnson's invitation I accompanied him as Aide, and the anomalous position we both occupied was frequently the subject of quiet jest between ourselves, but to outsiders we took hold of the command just the same as if it were ours by right, and never was a question raised by the gallant men whom it was our honor and privilege to lead to victory in the signal service they so conspicuously rendered on these bloody fields.

On the approach of Lee the doughty Pope was compelled to familiarize himself with another experience, to which, from his own account, he had hitherto been a stranger, to wit, to look after his lines of retreat, and he rapidly withdrew and recrossed the Rappahannock. As I now remember, there was some delay in our crossing the Rapidan in pursuit, a day or two, perhaps more, so that when we came up with him again he was found occupying strongly the crossings of the former stream. Time was exceedingly precious, as Burnside, with his troops, had already united and McClellan's troops were being hurried from the James to the Potomac and were arriving at Alexandria, while Porter had pushed forward and joined Pope.

Early, with his brigade, had crossed at Fauquier Springs, and a heavy rain had caused the river to rise and become unfordable, leaving him in an exposed and precarious position, from which he was only extricated by the incessant energy of our people in rebuilding the bridge, under the personal direction of General Jackson. Stuart, with his cavalry, had been thrown over the river, and, moving through Warrenton, struck the railroad immediately in Pope's rear at Catlett's

Station, capturing, in a night attack, a number of prisoners and Pope's headquarter wagon, with a lot of his personal effects and papers. Pope's uniform coat was afterward exhibited in Richmond. Stuart had barely escaped capture a few days before just below Orange Court House, being surprised while with his staff he was resting at a house on the roadside, waiting for his commands to come up, and in the confusion had lost his hat, which was carried off as a trophy to Pope. It was said he now proposed to Pope to exchange the latter's coat for his hat. Valuable papers fell into Stuart's hands at Catlett's, and his daring expedition but added to the federal consternation, and was another proof that lines of communication needed looking after. Among the prisoners captured I found an old friend, Captain Reinicker, of Baltimore, a former fellow-member of the Independent Greys.

General Lee then conceived the daring plan of turning Pope's right and throwing Jackson on his rear at Manassas, while he held the front with Longstreet's divisions on the Rappahannock. The story of this famed movement has gone into history. How by a rapid, forced march Jackson placed himself between Pope and Washington, capturing vast supplies of stores, trains of cars, batteries of artillery and destroying a command on the march from Alexandria to join Pope, and then drew off to a position on the Warrenton turnpike at about the old battlefield of July 21st, 1861, and calmly waited for Lee to come to his assistance. The audacity of this movement was unparalleled. Its effects were instantaneous and far-reaching. The federal authorities in Washington were in a state of panic, while Pope himself quickly let go his hold on the Rappahannock and moved his columns to crush Jackson before Longstreet could get to his relief. To use his own language, he confidently expected to "bag the whole crowd." The tactical movement made to accomplish this bagging operation culminated in his concentration on Manassas Junction, but the bird had flown, and his left was severely handled as they attempted to move along Jackson's front at Groveton on the evening of August 28th. The day we spent at Manassas Junction was a red-letter day in our experience.

We revelled in all sorts of army and sutler supplies. There were trainloads of meat, of bread and canned luxuries in plenty. With all our joy, there was an element of sorrow, that we had not the capacity for them all, and it was with heavy hearts we turned our backs on the profusion and marched across the country in the direction of the old battlefield. The following day found the brigade on the Warrenton turnpike at Groveton, with instructions to picket and hold that position from the expected advance of Pope from the direction of Gainesville and Haymarket. It was a rather lonesome position, as we did not know where the balance of the division was, it having moved from Manassas in the direction of Bull Run and Centreville. Early in the day we found the enemy approaching, and, making a show of our force, we opened upon them with our battery, and they quit the turnpike, moving to our left in the direction of the railroad. Later in the day the other brigades of the division, under General Taliaferro, came up and relieved our lonesomeness, and in the afternoon Ewell's division crossed at the Stone Bridge and all took position west of and facing the turnpike. Towards evening the enemy (King's division of McDowell's corps, with portion of Doubleday's division) advanced on the turnpike in force and a well-contested engagement followed, lasting until far into the night, without material advantage to either side. We held our ground, and after the action the enemy retired in the direction of Manassas Junction. In this engagement, which was participated in by three of Jackson's and two of Ewell's brigades, the confederate loss was quite heavy, Generals Ewell and Taliaferro both being wounded, the former losing a leg. In speaking of brigades, it must be borne in mind that the average strength of our brigades was 1000 to 1200 men at this period. King suffered a loss of about one-third of his command, so stubborn was the contest. Pope finding that Jackson was not at Manassas Junction, as he had supposed, but was resting on the turnpike south of the Stone Bridge, now directed his columns so as to place them between Washington and the confederate force, at the same time directing Porter's march so as to fall upon Jackson's right. He had also made dispositions, as he thought, to prevent the passage of Longstreet through the Bull Run mountains at Thoroughfare Gap, and hoped to bring on an engagement before the latter could unite with Jackson. Longstreet, however, successfully forced the passage of the mountain, and by noon on the 29th the head of his column came swinging along the road over which King had moved the preceding evening, and, taking position at Groveton, extended his right in the direction of the old battlefield. Porter, finding he could not execute Pope's order to attack Jackson's right without marching over the arriving divisions of Longstreet, wisely made a detour and united with Pope in Jackson's front. For this failure he was made the scapegoat, and after the battle relieved from command, then courtmartialed and cashiered. Some years after the close of the war he succeeded in having the case reopened, and, the testimony of confederate officers being then available, the impossibility of the execution of his orders was made apparent, and the decision of the former court reversed and he was restored to the army and placed on the retired list.

Early in the day of the 29th, Pope's dispositions for attack required Jackson to change his position of the 28th, and during the forenoon the skirmishing was quite heavy. Hill, with his division, held the left in the direction of Sudley Springs, while Jackson's and Ewell's divisions formed the right, reaching toward the turnpike, where Hood, forming Longstreet's left, was in position. Jackson had in his front a line of an old unfinished railroad, and along or in the rear of this his line was formed. Johnson's brigade, the 2d Virginia, was in line, slightly retired in a body of oak woods, the railroad referred to being in our front some 100 or 200 yards in an open field. The railroad grade was partly an embankment and partly a cut or excavation, while for a distance on our right it occupied the level. Towards noon the attack was made on Hill on our left, and a battle raged with great fury, but the federal assault was repulsed. The enemy then tried our line, and about 2 or 3 o'clock in the afternoon, after having massed in our front, protected from observation by the woods, moved to the attack in force, at the same time renewing the assault on Hill's lines. Our men were lying down resting when the firing commenced, and Colonel Johnson and myself, with other members of the brigade staff, were dismounted. Hill being somewhat nearer the enemy than ourselves, received the blow before we had any indication of the movement on our front. The attack was spirited, and in a little while there were indications of weakening on the part of the line on our immediate left. Colonel Johnson said to me he would go to the left and see how matters were progressing. The firing, shortly after he left, became much more violent, and a number of Hill's men came straggling back toward our line, and becoming somewhat apprehensive, I mounted my horse and had the brigade called up to "attention," when Johnson came running up the line, almost out of breath, and shouted to me: "Booth, charge them; they are upon us!" At that time we began to receive a scattering fire in our own front. Our line at the word moved forward, and Johnson, having mounted his horse, led them in the charge, driving back the federal skirmishers, who had already entered the woods in which we were posted, and as soon as we struck the open ground we came in contact with their advancing lines of battle. So impetuous was our charge, however, that they gave way, while we pursued them across the field and into the woods in which they had formed for the attack, capturing one piece of artillery and a number of prisoners. As we moved forward Gen. Charles W. Fields, with his brigade, and Stafford, with his Louisiana brigade, came to our support, and we did not halt our advance until the enemy was back to their original position and protected by their reserves. We then returned to our lines, bringing off with us the captured gun. As we entered our lines on our return, a staff officer from General Hood rode up and made inquiry as to the command that had made the "handsome charge." From the position at Groveton he had witnessed the movement and had full view, also, of the enemy in their advance.

August 29th closed with Jackson occuping the same lines he had assumed in the morning, every attack of the enemy having been repulsed with great loss. The night was spent under arms, the troops taking such rest as the situation would permit. We had now been engaged for two days, and our ranks had been thinned by casualties. A night under such circumstances is particularly trying on troops; the toils and labors of the day press hardly on their tired bodies, while the loss of comrades, with all the horrors and suffering which had attended their being disabled, now that the excitement of actual combat had subsided, was trying to the spirits of the bravest. Coupled with this was the certainty that the morrow's dawn would bring with it a resumption of the conflict, in which everyone was painfully sensible his turn might next come. About 9 o'clock at night Hood advanced his lines along the turnpike near Groveton, and met a body of the enemy, who were likewise advancing on our lines with a view of determining if we had not retreated, for by some insane infatuation Pope, notwithstanding his repulse all along our lines during the day, had conceived the idea that when we retired from the pursuit of his defeated columns, we had continued the movement and withdrawn from the field. Soon Hood's line and that of the enemy came in contact, and then ensued one of the prettiest sights of the war. From our position we could trace the respective lines by the light of the musketry fire, it being too dark to distinguish the troops themselves. The spitting fire of both the federal and confederate lines of battle just as plainly marked their position, however, as if it were in bright daylight. Hood's lines steadily advanced and the federal line slowly receded, and then the Texas yell rang out in the night and gave evidence that they were driving the foe. The object of the reconnaissance having been accomplished, about midnight, Hood returned to his position. At early daylight on the 30th we were up and on the alert. Skirmishing was going on all along our front, while our men were doing the best they could to prepare a meal. We still had a fair supply of the Manassas stores, including coffee, real sure-enough coffee.

The morning wore away without any indication of activity on the part of the enemy, and General Lee had abundant opportunity to inspect the field and establish his artillery in position, while Longstreet leisurely extended and strengthened his lines. Pope, in the meantime, having concentrated his army, was massing for an attack on Jackson's devoted lines. About 3 o'clock in the afternoon the attack was made in great force. In our immediate front we had heard the sounds of command as the troops were being massed in the woods for the attack, and when, under cover of heavy artillery fire from the federal batteries, they moved forward, as line after line of battle emerged from the woods and marched upon our position, the sight was magnificent. We did not propose this time to allow them to pass the railroad cut, but at once advanced and took position in or along the grade. As we moved forward to this position the fire of the enemy was severe and we lost heavily. Captain Goldsborough, of the old regiment, had joined us the preceding day, and Colonel Johnson had assigned him to one of the regiments of the brigade which was short of officers. In the movement to enter the cut he was badly wounded. As soon as we reached the cut we commenced firing and drove back line after line, but, notwithstanding the field in our front was covered with dead and wounded, the effect of our fire, there seemed to be no impression made on the advancing lines. The federals behaved with the greatest gallantry and marched steadily forward under our fearful fire, at the same time our artillery, under Col. Stephen D. Lee, was pouring into their exposed flank a most terrific storm of shot and shell. Still the steady and unremitting advance continued. At one time they actually reached the cut and entered it, while at one point, where there was a considerable embankment, their colors were held on the opposite side for some minutes, and the respective color-bearers, by inclining their staffs forward, could have made them touch. We knew not what was going on elsewhere, as our entire attention was occupied in beating back our immediate assailants. Soon our supply of ammunition commenced to fail, and, as a man was stricken down, the first thing was to strip off his cartridge box and distribute the cartridges. The line officers busied themselves in keeping their men supplied. Then came to our assistance the Louisiana brigade of Stafford, and the two commands mingled and kept up the struggle. At one time stones were actually hurled at the enemy on the other side of the railroad embankment, in the absence of ammunition.

In the rush forward for position in the cut, in passing some obstruction in the field, under the heavy fire I had become separated from Colonel Johnson and was with the left regiments of the brigade. At this time it was evident we could hold out but little longer in the absence of ammunition or assistance, and I asked Lieutenant Dunn, the Adjutant of the Irish Battalion, to go back and hurry forward a supply of the one or bring up the other. The open ground in our rear sloped upward to the woods from which we had moved, and in looking at this slope it seemed as if every square inch of soil was being torn by bullet or shell and nothing living could cross it. Dunn started to go, but the expression on his face clearly indicated he thought he was going to his death. I called him back and determined to try it myself. Following our line to our left until it reached the woods in which Hill was engaged, and thus avoiding the open field, I made my way back to some 100 yards or more in the rear of the position which we had occupied before the attack, and there, to my great joy, found a brigade in line, lying down. On enquiry, I was told it was Pender's brigade, and that officer was close at hand. I immediately made known to him our troubles and asked if he would not go forward to our assistance. He replied he had been sent there to support some one, he did not know who, and he could not see what was going on, but if I would show him the way he would go in to our relief. He immediately called up his brigade and moved forward, and, with a wild rush, charged over our exhausted lines in the cut, and the enemy not being able to stand this new development gave way and fled. In the meantime General Lee had directed Longstreet to advance and relieve the pressure on Jackson, and as Pender went forward, the right wing, under Longstreet, moved, driving the enemy in their front, and, in inclining to the left, closed in like a pair of shears on the now shattered and retreating foe, who retired in haste over Bull Run in great confusion. This movement of Longstreet closed the battle. The field was covered with dead, dying and wounded. The enemy had lost about 15,000 men, killed, wounded and prisoners, together with thirty pieces of artillery and more than 20,000 small arms. Our own loss was between 7000 and 8000 men, the larger part of which had been sustained by the divisions under Jackson. In the *melée* in the cut I received a slight wound in the thigh; the ball had evidently first struck an obstruction and only entered a part of its depth. It did not disable me from duty, but for some days the soreness was very inconvenient and I was quite feverish from its effect.

After crossing Bull Run, Pope took position at Centreville and was strengthened by the arrival of two corps from McClellan's army and Cox's division from Western Virginia, who had been hurried to the defense of Washington. General Lee did not propose, however, to allow him to rest, but on August 31st moved Jackson in the direction of the Little River turnpike, with a view of turning Pope's left, leaving Longstreet on the field to bury the dead and to secure the fruits of victory.

The movement of Jackson necessitated the relinquishing of the Centreville position, and Pope then sought to retire to the lines of the defenses at Alexandria. During the withdrawal the advance of Jackson assailed his line of march at Ox Hill, where a fierce combat ensued in the midst of a terrific thunderstorm, when the approach of darkness put an end to the strife, and the federal forces made good their retreat without further interruption. During this sanguinary action Gen. Phil. Kearney, a distinguished federal division commander, was killed.

Pope was now in the lines of the fortifications for the protection of Washington, and the command of the combined armies of the Potomac and of Virginia was assumed by McClellan, who addressed himself to the task of reorganizing the shattered forces, while Pope was left to the contemplation of his new and unpleasant experiences in the art of war, and was subsequently relegated to the northwest to look after the Indians. General Early, in an address before the Confederate Society in Baltimore in 1883, sarcastically said "Sitting Bull had not then made his appearance on the theatre of war, or we might never more have heard of Gen. John Pope."

General Lee now determined to cross the Potomac and put his column in motion through Leesburg, fording the river at White's Ferry, and on September 5th advanced on Frederick. The crossing of the Potomac was to Marylanders in the confederate service an incident of peculiar interest, and created in the army generally the wildest enthusiasm. It was hoped the accessions to our ranks would in a measure make good the losses of the campaign and our presence afford an opportunity to the people of Maryland to throw off the chains which had bound them in political servitude since the beginning of hostilities. In a most dignified address, General Lee presented to them the purpose of his movement, and gave assurance that no constraint would be placed on their independence of action. At the same time the most stringent orders were issued to the army, requiring respect to private property. Unfortunately the western section of the State was fairly evenly divided in sentiment, and the continuous presence of large bodies of federal troops had the effect of making the people overcautious and doubtful of the ability of the confederates in maintaining themselves and of affording adequate protection. The appearance of our men was not conducive to the inspiring of confidence. Instead of the well-equipped bodies of soldiery to which they had been accustomed, they now beheld the ragged, barefooted confederates, who appeared at their very worst. The losses of the summer campaign had depleted the ranks of our regiments, the hard marches had caused a fearful amount of straggling, and in every way the outward appearance was most unpromising. For weeks the men had subsisted on the most irregular issue of rations, and the corn fields had been resorted to for food. Green roasting ears are not to be despised, but for a constancy, without meat, salt or other condiment, their continued use is not altogether wholesome. The fierce rays of the midsummer sun and the consequent heat, with this poverty in supplies, had caused considerable sickness, and the poor feeble soldier, in his effort to keep up with his comrades in a strange land, presented a spectacle which, however much it appealed to the sympathy of the Marylander, did not inspire his confidence.

The crossing of the Potomac by Lee was followed by McClellan transferring his forces to Maryland also, and, under the pressure of the administration, he moved slowly in the direction of Frederick. The post at Harper's Ferry was garrisoned by a large federal force under Colonel Miles. While we were at Frederick it was reported to General Lee that this officer was still maintaining his position. This to General Lee was a matter of great surprise, as being contrary to all military prudence and principle. He said, on receiving this report, "Is it possible those people have not retired?" and at once made disposition to capture the force. This was successfully accomplished on the 15th, and 12,000 men, seventy pieces of artillery and large quantities of wagons, camp equipage, stores, etc., were surrendered to Jackson, who conducted the investment. While this movement was being executed, Lee moved Longstreet to the vicinity of Hagerstown, holding the crossings in the Blue Ridge with D. H. Hill's division and the cavalry. McClellan approached very slowly, entering Frederick some two days after Lee moved out, but here he came into possession of the general order which exposed to him the dispersed condition of the confederates. With this knowledge he was no longer in doubt as to his antagonist's position, and yet his natural caution and slowness of movement, together with a hearty respect for their prowess, prevented a hurried advance. He contented himself with forcing the passage of the mountains, which Hill defended until overwhelmed and driven out, and then took position on the Antietam, the west side of which, near Sharpsburg, was occupied by Lee, who was concentrating to meet the expected attack. Had the attack been made at once and in force, the result could not have failed but to have been disastrous to the confederate arms by reason of the meager force at hand ready for battle, but McClellan spent the 16th in getting ready. During the day Jackson, with the exception of A. P. Hill's division, reached Sharpsburg, after a forced march from the Ferry, where Hill had been left to parole the prisoners and secure the captured property. On the 17th the battle joined and raged throughout the entire day, the confederates maintaining their position, repulsing the successive attacks of the enemy, although at fearful cost. The thin lines were in places no more than skirmish lines, and at one time the federals had broken our right and reached within a few hundred yards of Lee's headquarters at the village on the main road leading to the river at Shepherdstown. At this critical moment the head of A. P. Hill's column came up and restored the broken confederate line, driving the enemy back to the Antietam on our right, while our left held on with unflinching tenacity. So closed the day. The Army of Northern Virginia fought Sharpsburg with not more than 35,000 men of all arms, and of these Hill only arrived late in the afternoon, just in time to save Lee's right. McClellan, by his own report, had 87,000 men, an excess of 52,000. It was possibly the hardest fought field of the war. The following day both armies maintained their positions, the confederates strengthening their lines, and stragglers coming up partly made good the losses of the preceding day. During the night General Lee retired to Virginia, crossing the river without molestation. McClellan made some show of pursuit by throwing two divisions of infantry over the river, when the rear, under Hill, turned upon them and drove them into the river with serious loss.

The Maryland campaign closed my service as an infantryman. Colonel Johnson had been appointed Provost-Marshal on arriving at Frederick, and General Jones having reported for duty, resumed the command of his brigade. We did not participate in the battle of Sharpsburg, but followed Jackson's march to Martinsburg in the operations on Harper's Ferry, and then rode to Richmond with important papers for the War Department. On arriving at Richmond we were met with the news of the battle and of Lee's return to Virginia. Being without a command, I was not averse to the opportunity for rest which now offered, and enjoyed a few days of recreation. While the army did not receive many accessions in upper Maryland, quite a number of our young men were crossing into Virginia over the lower Potomac, and as many of the members of the old regiment had gone to Richmond, several companies were being organized at this time and some had already gone to the front under Captains Herbert, Murray, Torsch and others, and a battalion organization was made at Winchester by the election of Capt. J. R. Herbert as Major, who very kindly tendered me the appointment as Adjutant. I went to Winchester to visit this command, and then explained to Major Herbert I had other purposes in view. During this week or more of my stay, I gave assistance in the drilling of the new companies, particularly Herbert's company, now commanded by Captain Duvall. Colonel Johnson had been so strongly recommended for promotion by General Jackson, and so much complimented by other officers of rank for the splendid manner in which he had handled the 2d brigade, that he confidently expected a commission as Brigadier-General, and at his request I held myself in readiness to take service on his staff. The President, however, at this time was very much embarassed by the demand to brigade the troops of each State as much as possible together and to assign brigade commanders on the same principle. Maryland had already so great a number of general officers, and no brigades for them to command, that the merit of Johnson could not find recognition, notwithstanding the endorsement and earnest appeal of General Jackson and others for his appointment. He was appointed, however, Colonel and assigned to duty as a member of a standing Military Court, while I had to look out elsewhere. I was fortunate to have open to me the hospitable home of Maj. William Greanor, at that time a wealthy citizen of Richmond and a former Baltimorean, and during the few weeks spent in Richmond Micawber-like, waiting for something to turn up, I experienced at his hand, and from his dear wife, every kindness in their power to bestow.

During the same summer an effort was made to organize a cavalry regiment of Marylanders. There was in the 1st Virginia Cavalry a company of Marylanders, commanded by Capt. G. R. Gaither. A number withdrew from this company, and, gathering up some additional material from those coming over, formed a new company, with Ridgely Brown, of Montgomery, as Captain, Frank A. Bond, of Anne Arundel, as 1st Lieutenant, with Thomas Griffith and J. A. V. Pue as 2d Lieutenants. This company had organized in the spring and had participated in the Valley campaign under Jackson, and was also with us in the seven days' battle around Richmond. During and after the Maryland campaign, other companies had been formed, and at this time a battalion had been organized, with Ridgely Brown as Major, and companies commanded by Captains Bond, Emack, Smith and Welch, to which were subsequently added companies under Captains Rasin, Schwartz and Hobbs, making up the 1st Maryland Cavalry, with Ridgely Brown, Lieutenant-Colonel, and R. Carter Smith, Major. While in Richmond I happened to meet my old friend, Capt. F. A. Bond, and he mentioned to me that Major Brown would be much pleased and gratified if I would accept the Adjutancy of the battalion. The proposition was agreeable to me. I was getting very tired of being away from the army and concluded to accept the offer. There was no delay in securing the appointment from the War Department, as my friend, Major Seddon, was in Richmond at the time, and at once offered to see his brother, the Secretary, and the commission was forthcoming at once. It was necessary, however, to get a mount, and here I was also fortunate to find an officer on General Huger's staff who was about going to the Trans-Mississippi and desired to sell out. I borrowed the money from a friend and paid $500 for horse and equipments. After bidding farewell to my good friends in Richmond, I started for the Valley to join the command in the latter part of 1862, stopping at Charlottesville to pay my respects to the family of ex-Governor Leake, who had been so kind and hospitable in the summer, when the old regiment was stationed near the town.

1863.

1863.

I reported to Major Brown near New Market, and was most heartily welcomed. It was like getting back to old friends again. The Valley District was at this time commanded by Brig.-Gen. W. E. Jones, with his cavalry brigade, together with the 1st Maryland Cavalry and the 2d Maryland Infantry, as it was hereafter known, and the Baltimore Light Artillery. These Maryland commands aggregated about 1000 men, the largest number of Marylanders that had been brought together since the beginning of the war. The enemy had position at Winchester and the intervening country was debatable ground. The iron furnaces at Edinburg produced a quality of iron which was particularly valuable to the Confederacy for ordnance purposes, and the entire product was devoted to the uses of the government. Whenever a sufficient quantity was turned out, the wagon trains would be sent to transport the same to the railroad at Staunton, and General Jones would move his command below Edinburg to protect the trains in this work; these frequent expeditions were termed as "pig iron raids." We were quartered in tents partly and in shelters made of brush, supplemented by tent flies or other cover as they could be improvised, and notwithstanding the cold weather and the poor character of shelter while in camp the general health of the men was excellent. The country was fairly stocked with supplies and there was plenty to eat, while the extras which were purchased from the thrifty farmers very materially added to our comfort and happiness. Our horses had a bountiful supply of long forage, as this was emphatically a grass-growing region, while there were large quantities of wheat, which was purchased by the Quartermaster at reasonable rates and converted into chop, upon which the horses grew fat, and when in the early spring the campaign opened, men and beasts were in good condition for service.

Not having experience in cavalry tactics, my spare time was largely consumed in study and fitting myself for the duties of my new position. The routine of office duties was familiar to me, and the returns of our command were soon placed on the regulation basis, to the great satisfaction of brigade headquarters. Several times during the winter we moved camp, and this, with the constant picket or outpost duty, gave occupation to the men, which served to dispel the monotony of a long and bitterly cold season. Major Brown was untiring in his efforts to bring his command to a state of efficiency, and his care for the comfort of the men, and the unvarying kindness with which he listened to their complaints, and looked after their general interests, soon made him beloved by all. He was ably supported by a number of his officers, who proved to possess exceptional merit, and when the campaign opened he had about 400 men, well mounted, fairly drilled and in the highest state of *morale*—a regiment that was destined to win renown in the cavalry service of the Confederacy and do honor to the State which it represented. Some of the officers were specially enterprising, among whom notably, Captain Bond. There was no better company commander in the army than this distinguished officer; gallant to a fault, firm in his discipline and control of men, while his intelligence and natural soldierly abilities, now developed by two years' active service and experience, well fitted him as a leader. Captain Emack had personal gallantry to a degree that he was absolutely without fear. I have often thought that a body of 1000 cavalry, made up of such men as Emack, would ride down any opposition and execute any order given them, at least until they were all dismounted or disabled. He did not possess the judgment or all-around qualities that marked Captain Bond, but in personal courage had no superior in the army.

Captain Smith had served as a Captain in the 1st Maryland Infantry, he was cool and collected in action, of undoubted bravery and possessed all the qualities of a gentleman. His only weakness as a cavalry commander came from his being too indulgent to his men and not enforcing discipline as strictly as good order and complete efficiency required. Captain Welsh was another beau-ideal cavalryman. He was always in the front and in the lead. His natural genius made him prominent in action, in fact, he was stronger in personal execution and leadership than in commanding or directing others. Captain Rasin was our youngest company commander. He combined, with dash and personal courage of a high type, unquestioned ability and power to command. Later on, Captain Schwartz joined with his company. This officer had the advantage of previous training in Major Brown's own company, and bid fair to make a most efficient and capable officer. His early death, the result of wounds, cut short his promising career. Such was the *personnel* of the company commanders who under the gallant and loved Brown were destined to make the command conspicuous for devotion, efficiency and reliability and acquire a fame and reputation which was recognized throughout the entire cavalry corps of the Army of Northern Virginia.

Lieutenant-Colonel Herbert was just as fortunate in the support given him in organizing and perfecting his command, the 2d Maryland Infantry. He had the gallant Goldsborough, a born soldier; the noble Murray, that paladin of gentle graces, with irreproachable courage and ability to command men, and the veteran Torsch, whose training and experience made him extremely valuable. These had experience as company commanders before the organization of their present command, and with the remaining Captains, who were somewhat new to their present duties, but who soon acquired the knowledge under the schooling of Herbert and the others, made the 2d Maryland Infantry a well-ordered and efficient command. A number of the subaltern officers, as well as the men themselves, had served in the old regiment, and their example helped to develop the soldierly qualities of the new men. Colonel Herbert had a gift for organization and system. He knew the necessity of discipline and had been taught himself the duties of a soldier by no less proficient an officer than Gen. George H. Steuart, our old Colonel.

As spring opened Herbert had about 600 well-drilled, well-clothed and properly-equipped men to lead forth to service and to mark out for themselves a record of glory second to no regiment in the army, and to win from General Lee himself the title of the "gallant battalion." From Gettysburg, where they left one-half of their number in the enemy's lines on Culp's Hill, to Cold Harbor, Petersburg, Weldon Railroad and finally to the last sad day at Appomattox, they bore the colors of the State and made a record of which Maryland will ever be proud so long as fortitude, devotion, honor and courage are honored by an admiring people.

In March, while the brigade was encamped near Edinburg, Bond and his company were on outpost duty near Fisher's Hill. His instructions were merely to picket the front and advise of any threatened advance or other movement of the enemy, who, under Milroy, with a division of infantry and several regiments of cavalry, occupied Winchester. Bond, however, was not satisfied with this mere performance of duty, and he concluded to strike out on his own account. He moved his company forward on what was called the Back road to within a few miles of Winchester, and then striking across the country until he reached the main road of the Valley turnpike, not far from Kernstown, when, finding himself between Winchester and the enemy's outposts, he proceeded to capture their pickets and bring them off. This, under the very shadow of their camp, brought on him, as soon as the alarm was sounded, their cavalry in force, and some two regiments followed him in close pursuit, which did not stop when our outposts were reached, but continued and threatened to endanger our very camp. Then came messengers from Bond to warn us of the rapid approach of the enemy. Our men were scattered, engaged in various duties or pleasures, not dreaming of any hostile force being within thirty miles. Herbert gave the alarm by beating the long roll, the men in the cavalry camps saddled up their horses and mounted, and without any attempt toward formation, went down the road to the front, while those out of camp hurried back and were speedily formed and moved toward the approaching enemy. General Jones, with what men he could gather, made effort to hold the enemy in check, but they pushed forward with great vigor, and at one time it looked as if Bond had stirred up a hornet's nest to plague us, but as soon as our commands were gathered into some formation, although not strong in numbers by reason of the hurry and confusion in which they were turned out, they moved to the support of General Jones, who at once took the offensive and charged the federals in front and in flank, driving them back pell-mell through Tom's Brook and Strasburg, not halting the pursuit until they were in shelter of their main body. The same physic they gave Bond and his men was given them back in profuse doses. We captured between two and three hundred of them, with many horses, and the affair, which at one time had an ugly look for us, was converted into a brilliant success. I remember, however, Bond was not particularly anxious to meet General Jones and report how the matter had been brought about, and we privately speculated what would have been his fate if the result had been a disaster. General Jones, "Old Grumble Jones," as he was called in the old service, was a disagreeable customer when crossed, and his temper and forbearance would have been severely tested if, by this infraction of discipline or movement without orders, his command had suffered a reverse. As it was, our success was so pronounced that Captain Bond got off with a mild scolding.

After this episode matters quieted down, until April 21st, 1863, when General Jones, with his entire command, except a small force left in the Shenandoah Valley to observe the enemy, started on his famous West Virginia raid. His forces, consisting of about 2500 well-mounted cavalry, the 2d Maryland Infantry and the Baltimore Light Artillery, moved westward, crossed the North Mountain range and took the direction of Moorefield. The roads were soft from the breaking up of winter, and were made worse by the April rains, which set in about the time of starting, making the march through the mountains particularly gloomy and uncomfortable. The vicinity of Moorefield, Hardy County, was reached in the afternoon of the 24th, when we found our further progress was interrupted by the high waters of the South Branch, which prevented our crossing at that point. Colonel Herbert, with the infantry and the artillery, was left at Moorefield, while the brigade moved the next day up the river to the vicinity of Petersburg, where a crossing was effected with considerable difficulty and some loss. The raging stream was out of its banks, with a swift current, which buffeted the men as they plunged in and essayed to make their way in the flood. A number of men and horses were swept away, but the orders were imperative to move forward. The courage and hardihood that were put to this test was a new experience to most of us, and not a few who would have unflinchingly faced a charging column or a heavy fire without question, hesitated when their turn came to enter the angry stream and risk their lives in a contest with the enraged forces of nature. Several hours were consumed in this movement, and when night fell it found the command on the western bank of the Potomac. On going into camp for the night the first thing to be looked after was the care of our wearied horses. In the neighboring meadows were several large stacks of hay, and Colonel Brown directed the men to help themselves. On reaching one of these stacks it was found to be under the protection of a squad from one of the regiments of the brigade, who claimed they had orders from Colonel Lomax not to permit it to be disturbed save by their own people. A contention then ensued, which at one time bid fair to end in trouble, but our men came down in force and took possession, and in a little while the noble proportions of the stack were sensibly marred to the immediate advantage of our hungry steeds. Early in the morning the columns were reformed and took the road toward New Creek, now Keyser, a prominent station on the B. & O. R. R. In the course of the afternoon we entered what is known as Greenland Gap, and in a little while the head of the column struck a federal picket post, which was promptly driven in and several of the pickets captured. Their main body consisted of two infantry companies, about 100 men, who took refuge in a log church, which occupied a position immediately alongside the main road, with a small clearing of perhaps an acre about it. On the other side of the road the mountain rose abruptly and the narrow passageway or defile was completely commanded by the church. Col. Richard Dulany, with his regiment, the 7th Virginia, had the advance, followed in column by the 1st Maryland. Colonel Dulany at once concluded to force the passage, and charged the church, receiving from it a heavy and well-directed fire, which broke his regiment, himself being badly wounded. A portion of his men succeeded in getting by, but the remainder, consisting of the larger portion, were driven back. General Jones then considered the measures to be adopted to clear the way. We knew perfectly well the force that was in the church, and Dulany's men, who had ridden through the fire, prevented any withdrawal or retreat had they so desired, but their commander, Capt. Martin Wallace, 23d Illinois, a gallant fellow, had but little idea of forsaking his post. He was summoned to surrender, and one of his own men, whom we had captured, was shown our column and told of our force and then dispatched to his Captain with the message that if he persisted in defending his position against overwhelming numbers, thereby causing unnecessary loss of life, he would, by the rules of war, forfeit right to quarter and consideration, as we were determined to assault his position if he would not yield. The man came back to us with his Captain's reply, that if we wanted him we would have to "come and take him," and if any more such messengers were sent he would shoot them down as they approached, at the same time stimulating the return by the application of his boot to the nethermost part of the anatomy of our "flag." Then it was we sadly missed our battery. One gun of the Baltimore Light Artillery would have settled the controversy in a few moments, but that gun was twenty miles away over the river at Moorefield. It was then proposed we should form a storming column, taking powder and endeavor to blow up the church. This, after consideration, was abandoned as being possibly as dangerous to our people as to the enemy. Finally, some time after dark, General Jones, who had grown very impatient at the prolonged delay, directed Colonel Brown to dismount his leading squadrons and to take inflammable matter with which to fire the church, while he beat in the doors and windows and took the enemy out. We gathered the men, who had revolvers and carbines, and, forming them in column of fours, supported by White's battalion which had joined in with us, started at a run for the church. The night was bright with the light of a brilliant moon, which lit up the road and the rugged mountain sides with a weird, cold brightness. The road was crossed between our point of starting and the church several times by a stream, at that time partly full from the recent rains and about knee deep, and the water was of that icy temperature that our garments became stiffly frozen as quickly as we emerged from the stream. As soon as the turn of the road brought us in range of the church the federals commenced their fire on our devoted columns, and it was not until we reached the building itself that we were momentarily protected, because they could not depress their guns as we closed around its walls, but this immunity lasted but for a minute or two. In the rush Captain Bond and myself started in company, but I tripped over a stone or some such object in the road, which threw me back some little, and we became separated. When I reached the church it was at the door, and I found Colonel Brown at one side, while several of our men were directing heavy blows with axes in their effort to force an opening. We could not see anything of our foes, as they were inside under secure cover. I placed my back to the walls, so as to be out of range of the fire from the windows, when a blow on my shoulder forced me forward and half around, and a blaze of fire passed my face as I realized the enemy were now on the ground floor and were thrusting their guns between the logs of the wall of the church, forcing out the chinking, and that it was the muzzle of a musket, thus thrust through, that had pushed me out of the line of its destructive fire. From this condition there was no escape, and here we lost heavily, the ground soon being covered with our fallen. Almost instinctively I moved from this dangerous position, and had proceeded not more than a few feet along the side of the house, when I was shot in the thigh and a heavy thud brought me to my knees. In this position I remained a few moments, while the work of destruction was going on and our boys were falling all around under a fire they could not return. The blows of the axes were still ringing on the doors and windows, but, what was more comforting was a small blaze, which now appeared at the far corner of the church, the light from which lit up the fearful surrounding and told us it would soon force the enemy out. At this juncture the door gave way, and in sprang our Sergeant-Major, Edward Johnson, pistol in hand, and called upon the commanding officer to surrender. The door was again closed, with Johnson on the inside. The flames and smoke, however, now had their effect, and from the inside of the house came cries for quarter, while our men forced their way in and brought out the defenders. All this time I felt the blood as it freely flowed from my wounded thigh and filled the leg of my boot, and calling to one of the men, I asked him to walk off with me, as I was hurt. I rose to my feet and staggered away, crossing the stream, which ran not twenty yards from the church, when I fell and lost consciousness. I recall distinctly, however, the sight that was around the building as I moved off. The ground was fairly covered with our dead and wounded, the flames were leaping up and enveloping the church, while through the now open doorway I could see the federals as our men were dragging them out. But few of the enemy were shot, not more than three or four, and these in the *melée* above described. They had fairly forfeited their right to quarter, but our men recognized their gallantry and forebore to inflict a punishment which the circumstances might have justified. I was carried back to the point from which we had made the assault, and the house on the roadside was soon filled with the wounded, including Colonel Brown, Captain Smith, Lieutenants Pue and Beatty and myself. Immediate preparations were made to continue the march, the prisoners being dispatched to Moorefield, where they were turned over to Colonel Herbert. As our wounds were being dressed, the marching on the roadside indicated we were being left behind, and the prospect of falling into the hands of the enemy became a burning question. I felt pretty well assured that during the following day the enemy from New Creek would reoccupy the Gap and would send back those they found wounded.

Lieutenant Pue was wounded in his shoulder and was not disabled from riding his horse, which had been left behind for his use. Lieutenant Beatty and myself were so badly hurt as not to be able to ride, and our horses were carried on with the command. Captain Smith was badly wounded in the arm, but was able to ride back to Moorefield. Colonel Brown determined to accompany the command, but in a few days his injuries compelled him to retire. Lieutenant Pue was summoned, and I asked him to cause a horse to be hitched to an old vehicle, which I had observed under a shed, as we were considering the ways and means of the attack during the afternoon, and as soon as it was light we were loaded into it and started for Moorefield, accompanied by William Webster, of Bond's company, who had been detailed to look after our wants. A long, weary day of intense suffering followed. The rough mountain roads jarred and jolted our poor wounded bodies so that at times we felt we could proceed no further, but the anxiety to escape prison called up all the fortitude and reserve strength at our command, and we persevered, until towards the close of the afternoon we neared Moorefield, when information was received that Herbert had left and the enemy was in the vicinity. This led us to move higher up the river, some four or five miles distant, where we effected a crossing, and about nightfall were met in the road by a citizen, to whom we gave our story and asked him where we could find shelter for the night. Under God's providence we had met with one of the noblest of His handiwork, and the cordial invitation to go to his home and the welcome we there received, and the hospitable attention and tender nursing for many weeks which was bestowed upon us by Mr. Solomon Van Meter and his estimable wife, will never be forgotten. A physician from Moorfield treated our wounds, which, painful as they were, yielded to our young and vigorous constitutions. Lieutenant Pue continued on to Harrisonburg, leaving Mr. Webster to look after Beatty and myself. The enemy were frequently in the neighborhood, but so carefully was our secret kept, and so discreet and prudent Mr. Van Meter's family, and so true and faithful were his servants, that we were not discovered or disturbed.

Whilst lying on our backs at Mr. Van Meter's came the news of Chancellorsville and the death of Jackson. This last, to us, was the saddest intelligence that could come to mortal ears, as, with the loss of this great soldier, to whom we were so endeared, came the fearful apprehension that there was no one to make good to the cause the place he had so signally filled with such brilliant success. Well might General Lee, who knew and appreciated his ability and worth better than any other, write to Jackson that "could he have directed events he would have chosen to have been disabled in his stead," and afterward, in commenting on the sad termination, in a letter to Mrs. Lee, "I know not how to replace him, but God's will be done; I trust He will raise some one to take his place."

After leaving us at Greenland, General Jones proceeded on his expedition through West Virginia, following the line of railroad as far as Oakland, thence to Morgantown, then to Fairmont, and from thence to Clarksburg and Bridgeport, then following the line of the Parkersburg Branch to Cairo and Oil City on Kanawha, gathering supplies of cattle, horses and provisions, which were sent back to the confederate lines. At Oil City was found immense quantities of petroleum, which was then coming largely into commercial use. The oil was in barrels, by the thousands, and in bulk in boats; the torch was applied, and as the burning fluid spread itself over the surface of the waters the old General was heard to exclaim, "Well, they said I would never set a river on fire; what do you call that?" After destroying the railroad at several points, the head of the column was turned homeward and returned to the vicinity of New Market, reaching the main Valley some time in the latter part of May.

About the middle of June our wounds had improved, and the incursions of the enemy to Moorefield and the South Branch Valley became so frequent and threatening that Lieutenant Beatty and myself concluded it was no longer safe to remain in our hospitable quarters, and we arranged to be carried into our lines, reaching Harrisonburg after a rather trying journey. I continued on to Charlottesville, where, in the latter part of the month, Colonels Johnson and Brown arrived *en route* for the army, which had left the Fredericksburg lines and had moved down the Valley, driving Milroy out of Winchester, making valuable captures of material and stores, and was then in the act of crossing the river into Maryland. Although my wound was yet unhealed, the enthusiasm of a prospective campaign in Maryland and Pennsylvania led me to overestimate my strength, and I insisted on accompanying them. The imprudence of this procedure soon became manifest, and frequently my enfeebled condition required a halt and rest on the roadside, but those dear comrades, filled as they were with anxiety to reach the front, where such stirring events were being enacted, never lost patience, but tenderly cared for me, without any outward evidence of the disappointment which the delay was causing to them. In a few days, however, I became more seasoned to the fatigue, and we were able to make a fair day's journey. On reaching the river at Shepherdstown we ascertained the army was all over and had entered Pennsylvania. The country on the Virginia side, however, was filled with straggling cavalrymen who had not been able to accompany their commands by reason of being on detached service when they had moved, or had remained behind to have their horses shod, and, like us, were trying to rejoin their commands. Colonel Johnson gathered together some several hundred of these men, quite a regiment in numbers, and then crossed the river, proceeding through Sharpsburg and the battlefield at that point, with the purpose of passing through Hagerstown. When within a few miles of this place we met two gentlemen in a buggy.

just out from the town, who informed us the federals were in possession, whereupon we struck over to the Greencastle road and entered that town after nightfall. Johnson required the citizens to supply the men with food, very much to the distress of some of them, whose familiarity with the hardships of war had been confined to the newspaper accounts of the acts of their own people in Virginia, which were now to be pressed home upon them in a manner not at all agreeable. One party, I recall, protested very strongly against our demands, and stated in his justification, and as an evidence that he had already been despoiled to a degree that was positively horrifying and alarming, that when the army had passed that way the previous week they had actually taken from him one entire week's baking of bread. This piteous plea did not find appreciation from men who had experienced the desolation of Pope and of Milroy, and the oppressed citizen was given to understand he had better find the means to make his contribution without further delay. Nothing was disturbed, however, in the way of personal property. All we asked for was food, and in that land of plenty this worked no particular hardship.

The next day we marched to Chambersburg, where we met up with General Imboden, with his brigade, and our improvised command was turned over to him. He hospitably entertained us over night, and gave the information that we would probably find the main army in the neighborhood of Gettysburg. At early dawn we started out to ride to that town. Our party consisted of Colonels Johnson and Brown, one private, Colonel Johnson's negro servant Jacob, and myself, and for some thirty miles we rode through the enemy's country without seeing any of our troops, passing through many settlements *en route*, filled with hundreds of men, who stared at us, but did not offer the slightest molestation. I do not think such a party of federals could have made a similar journey in Virginia; the very boys would have taken them in hand. As we reached the vicinity of Cashtown, we met up with Pickett's division *en route* for Gettysburg, and had halted on the roadside for rest, their arms being in stacks on the turnpike. As this was the first body of confederate infantry we had met since overtaking the army, we were somewhat interested as to their strength. I made a rough count or estimate from the stacked guns, and remember distinctly we reached the conclusion they numbered about 4,500 men. Within a mile or two of Gettysburg we met Colonel Chilton, General Lee's Adjutant-General, who had just finished paroling some thousands of prisoners, the captures of July 1st, the preceding day, and in a short while we rode over the battlefield of that action, which had resulted in the utter defeat of the 1st and 11th corps and Buford's cavalry. On reaching Gettysburg we found our troops in possession, Ewell's line of battle running through a portion of the town, while the enemy was occupying Cemetery hill, with a line reaching from Culp's hill on their right to Little Round Top on their left. We reported to General Ewell, and Colonel Johnson was informed that the Maryland Line, which he had expected to command, had been distributed. Herbert, with the infantry, having been assigned to Steuart's brigade of Johnson's division, the artillery being separated and assigned to several battalions, while the cavalry was engaged on various duties, one squadron, under Captain Bond, being at corps' headquarters. Colonel Brown at once started off to look after his scattered command, while Colonel Johnson and myself remained with General Ewell, and thus had an opportunity of observing the movements in that quarter. The fatigue of the long ride from Charlottesville, in my wretched physical condition, rendered me unfit for continuous or regular duty, although fortunately no serious trouble was experienced from my still open wound.

I do not propose to say much as to Gettysburg. From the extreme left, where we spent the evening of the second and the third day of the fight, we could not see the movements on our right, as, owing to the formation of the lines of battle, a straight line from our left to our right would have crossed the federal rear centre. I witnessed, however, the assault made by Ewell on Cemetery hill, where Early and Hays, in a hand-to-hand contest, succeeded in gaining the hill and the guns, only to be driven back for want of proper support. I also witnessed the remarkable cannonade in which some 200 pieces of artillery joined, preparatory to Pickett's magnificent charge, and when our advancing lines were broken and driven back I witnessed the heroism and confident obedience with which our men reformed and held their position, with the utter absence of anything like demoralization or evidence of defeat. The truth is, our people had implicit confidence in General Lee and their own ability to whip the enemy under anything like fair conditions, and when, to their great surprise, they failed to take the federal position, it never occurred to them there was the slightest danger from any attack in return. They felt absolutely able to take care of anything of that character. In the early days of the war, I have understood that General Lee was not altogether hopeful of results from the illy-organized volunteer troops. As the army under his direction and skillful leadership developed their fighting power and ability to win great victories under the most adverse circumstances, and in spite of the large numbers opposed them, his appreciation of their prowess and admiration of their gallantry and soldierly qualities rose to a measure of confidence which, perhaps, led him to movements which, with more indifferent material, he would never had undertaken. Thus the apprehensions of the early days became converted into a feeling that nothing was impossible with these men, who followed him with such affection and complete confidence. Lee was a bold soldier, a master of strategy and a vigorous fighter. The great preponderance of numbers and appliances with which he had to contend could not be met by the usual caution with which great military operations are ordinarily conducted. Great risks were necessarily assumed, and he felt the Army of Northern Virginia was equal to all demands which he might be called upon to subject it. Even at this late day it does not appear he was mistaken or unjustified in this excellent opinion of his troops. The testimony of a former adversary who fell under his mailed hand and their heavy blows, styled them as the most "incomparable body of infantry" the world had ever seen. Unfortunately, there was lacking that intelligent, unhesitating support such as he received from Jackson. There are but few confederates who will not solemnly assert that, in their judgment, had Jackson been at Gettysburg on the evening of July 1st, history would have to look elsewhere for the signal chapters for which the events of the two successive days furnished such sad material. Mutual overconfidence, the General in his troops, and they in him and their own power, together with a fearful lack of prompt, energetic obedience on the part of those occupying high places, tell the story of the failure. But even in defeat did the strength of the grand hero and his noble army appear brightest. Upon himself he took the responsibility and blame which attached to others. "Never mind men, it is all my fault," while they, with sullen and dogged steps, moved back to the new positions, without any appearance of disorder or demoralization.

During the action of July 3d my horse was struck by a piece of shell, and for a moment I thought I had been hit myself, as the frightened animal reared and pitched, his blood coursing like fire through his veins, which peculiar and heated sensation extended to my own person. The damage sustained was slight, not sufficient to disable him. On July 4th it became apparent we would retire during the night, and I paid a visit to the wounded of the 2d Maryland Infantry. Herbert had carried 400 muskets into the fight; they now numbered less than 200, and those that were not left in the federal lines on Culp's hill had been gathered into the hospitals which were established in almost every barn or house in our rear. With deep sadness I took what was thought to be the last farewell of Herbert and Goldsborough, whose wounds seemed to forbid any hope of recovery. Recover they did, however, the first to fill posts of honor and usefulness in after years in our own city, and the latter is still with us in the flesh.

Colonel Johnson, after the battle, was assigned to the command of the 2d brigade, the same one he had commanded with so much distinction at Second Manassas, and I saw very little more of him until our return to Virginia. I remained with Captain Bond, who, with his company, held Ewell's position on the withdrawal of the army on the night of July 4th, while Colonel Brown, with what he could gather of the regiment, was engaged in the protection of our trains, which were being assailed at all points by federal cavalry. The slow movement of the trains and troops on the night of the 4th in their withdrawal made it toward morning on the 5th when the rear of Ewell's corps left their position. Bond at once threw out his company as videttes and occupied the ground, advancing somewhat to the enemy, who made no effort to move forward until some considerable time after the day opened, when the road having been cleared, we withdrew finally, being the last confederates to leave the field. On joining the column at Fairfield, Bond was instructed to hurry towards Hagerstown, where our trains were endangered by the enterprise of the enemy's cavalry. Meade's advance or offensive movement was entirely confined to the efforts of his cavalry to break into our long extended wagon trains, but even this did not meet with very much success, as our losses in this quarter were insignificant. Pushing rapidly forward, Bond reached Hagerstown, through which our trains were moving to Williamsport. No infantry had as yet come up, but the firing in the direction of Williamsport indicated that the enemy's cavalry were making things lively at that point. Early in the afternoon the enemy approached Hagerstown on the Baltimore turnpike, and the 10th Virginia Cavalry, under Col. J. Lucius Davis, who were out on that road, were driven in just as we were moving down Potomac street. Bond held his men in the middle of the street, in column of fours, the fleeing cavalrymen riding by us on either side, until we were threatened with being overwhelmed by them in their flight. We then wheeled about and retired, hoping to extricate ourselves from the runaway mob. The rapid pursuit of the enemy, however, brought their charging columns into the town, and in a moment they were at our heels. The street had by this time become cleared of all except our command, and Bond at once gave the order "Fours right about" just in time to bring us facing and in contact with the charging column. At the word we dashed forward to meet their onset; the sabre was freely used. Sergt. Hammond Dorsey, whose position was on the left of the company, by this right about movement was thrown in front, and as soon as he fairly turned, went to work with his sabre, and some five or six federals fell under his rapid blows. The unexpected had happened, and the federal column, finding themselves so vigorously assailed, turned and fled, our men pursuing them for some little distance beyond the college, which was on the edge of the town. This gallant action on the part of Captain Bond and his command saved our trains, which were unprotected and strung out on the turnpike, and in a little while the head of our infantry column entered the town, and there was no more danger on that score. From Hagerstown to Williamsport, however, a distance of six miles, the trains occupied the road, and the enemy were persistent in their efforts to break in on them; in fact, there was a constant skirmish going on all along the line until late in the afternoon. Stuart, with his cavalry, cleared our flanks of these disagreeable and troublesome people. Toward night Bond was severely wounded during one of these *melées*, and was carried to Hagerstown. On the retirement of the army he could not be moved, and fell into the hands of the enemy, not being exchanged until toward the close of the war, and thus was lost to the regiment the service of this most capable and gallant officer.

The heavy rains which had set in after the battle caused the Potomac to rise, and our pontoons gave way, cutting off communication with the Virginia shore. The river being unfordable, General Lee was forced to suspend his movement for several days, and he took position just south of Hagerstown and waited for Meade to attack. There was no uneasiness among the men; on the contrary, they were rather hopeful that an attack would be made and an opportunity afforded to repay the debt which they had contracted at Gettysburg. They did not know that the supply of ammunition had run so low as not to be sufficient for a prolonged engagement, and this anxiety, which so oppressed General Lee, did not affect their spirits. In blissful ignorance while they waited for the attack, General Lee addressed every effort to bring over the river ammunition and to relay the pontoons, but it was not until the night of July 13th that sufficient progress had been made and the waters had subsided so as to enable him to resume the withdrawal and recross the river. Meade called his corps commanders together in council, but they advised against an attack. In the meantime he was being cruelly urged by the authorities in Washington not to permit Lee to escape, and when, under this incessant prodding, he determined to move out on the morning of the 14th to make a reconnoissance in force, with a view of converting into an attack if the result justified, he found his antagonists had left nothing but the embers of their camp fires to mark the lines, and the rear of the covering cavalry was some distance out on the Williamsport road. We were at once pressed, and had scarcely made good our crossing when the enemy came down to the river and exchanged shots. Everything was gone clean and clear. At Falling Waters, where the larger part of the army crossed over on the bridge, Meade did advance and succeed in capturing some prisoners, mostly stragglers, and in the effort to save these men General Pettigrew was killed. General Lee emphatically denied having sustained any such losses as claimed by the federals.

Upon Meade's conveying to the Washington authorities the intelligence that Lee had returned to Virginia, Halleck wired him the President was much disappointed and could not restrain the conviction that the pursuit had not been sufficiently active. Under this implied censure, Meade asked to be relieved, but apologies and explanations were made and he remained in command. In his testimony before the Congressional Military Committee, considerably later on, he said that he was convinced that if he had made the attack on Lee in the Hagerstown lines, the result would have been disastrous to the federal arms. This evidence from the commander of the Army of the Potomac is in itself a sufficient tribute to the army of Lee, and clearly shows the wholesome respect in which their adversaries held their prowess, even after the severe losses at Gettysburg. After the return to Virginia there was for a week or more a period of rest, but on the movement of Meade into Loudoun and thence to Fauquier General Lee left the Valley and took position at Culpeper, behind the Rappahannock. Soon after he withdrew to the line of the Rapidan. The Maryland cavalry was then assigned to the brigade of Fitz Lee, and took position on the extreme right, near Fredericksburg, camping on Marye's hill. The federal cavalry occupied the Stafford side of the river, and in plain view we could see their movements as they went down the "Neck," returning with supplies, etc. For some time we had a good rest; the only serious trouble we experienced arose from the want of grain for our horses. There was no hay in the country, and we had to fall back on the poor supply of natural grass which this rather impoverished section meagerly furnished, supplemented now and then by a small issue of corn. Personally, our greatest discomfort was from the mosquitoes, and after a considerable experience with this pest from the Panama isthmus to a very long residence in Tidewater Virginia, I can conscientiously state that those encountered on the banks of the Rappahannock just below Fredericksburg, as we picketed and patrolled the river during these August nights, were the vilest, most ravenous and bloodthirsty of their kind. To relieve the monotony of these days, reviews were held of the brigade, now commanded by General Wickham, who succeeded Fitz Lee when the latter was made Major-General and a division commander. We also got up an expedition to cross the river and stir up the enemy, hoping to catch some of them out from their main body with wagons, which we might destroy, if not capture and bring over. This expedition was made up of 100 men of the 3d Virginia, under Colonel Owen, and 100 men of the 1st Maryland, under my command. We proceeded down the river to Port Conway, some twenty miles below Fredericksburg, where we effected a crossing by swimming the horses, carrying the men over in small boats. Without much trouble we got over in good shape, and then started up the river, through King George, and about dusk had reached a point some three or four miles below Falmouth, just opposite Fredericksburg, but without meeting any of the foraging parties as we had hoped. Colonel Owen then directed me to take the advance with my detachment and move quietly along the river road, picking up the enemy's pickets, and make for the ford at Falmouth, where we were to cross to the Fredericksburg side. It was now quite dark, and across the river we could see the fires of our camps and hear the bugles as they sounded taps. I entrusted the advance to Christopher Billopps, with several men, who kept some fifty or 100 yards ahead of the column, and soon began to pick up the unsuspecting pickets along the river bank. All was going on well, when there was heard a volley in our rear, where Colonel Owen was following with his detachment; then followed more firing, and I knew there was no longer anything for us to hope for but a rapid movement over the river. The enemy had a division of cavalry camped not more than a mile or two from the river, and the alarm being given, by the time we could reach the ford they would be upon us. At once we started the trot, and as we advanced had sensible evidence that the enemy were aroused, as we were being fired upon from all directions except from over the river, where the commotion in our own camps showed how our friends were being disturbed by the firing.

It did not take very long to make the ford, I am sure, but to me it seemed we would never reach the desired spot. Finally, the road turned down toward the river, and without drawing rein, in we plunged and then found our horses swimming, the tide being still at flood, but over we went, and on reaching the other side I at once formed along the river to cover Colonel Owen, as, in like manner, he made good his crossing. He was not far behind me, and in a few minutes we were all safely over, while a perfect hornet's nest of enraged federal cavalry were riding down to the ford and all along the river bank and over the country from which we had emerged. On our side of the river the troops had been turned out, and all was agog with excitement. We had the satisfaction of knowing that we had made it pretty lively on both sides of the river for one night, even if we had no good result to show for our raid. As it was, we brought over with us some ten or twelve prisoners. I have always thought that the firing that gave us away was from our own men, some of whom in the darkness had taken a road (the country was a perfect network of roads made by federals in their long occupation) which led them by a longer route than that followed by the main column, which they struck in the rear as their path re-entered the main road. However it happened, the jig came very near being up with us.

The early part of October found us in the vicinity of Morton's Ford and under the command of Gen. L. L. Lomax, who had recently been made a Brigadier-General. It had become necessary to strengthen the army under General Bragg in Tennessee, and Longstreet, with two of his divisions, had been dispatched to that section. Meade also sent a portion of his army to the west, but still largely outnumbered Lee, who nevertheless determined to advance, with a view of giving battle. As our cavalry crossed the Rapidan at Morton's Ford, driving the enemy before us, the infantry were moved in the direction of Madison Court House. Meade, finding his right had been turned, became apprehensive for his line of supplies, and having doubtless the experience of Pope in the previous year as a lesson before his eyes, rapidly withdrew across the Rappahannock. Our cavalry, under Stuart, Hampton and Fitz Lee, kept up a running fight with the federal cavalry until the latter found refuge in the infantry lines between Brandy station and the river. Whilst our division was engaged in pressing the enemy near Brandy station our attention was directed to a considerable commotion in our rear, and we then found a heavy body of the enemy's cavalry was coming down upon us from the direction of Culpeper Court House. They spread out over the country, and were advancing at a rapid gait, and for a while it looked as if we had been caught between their forces and were in danger of being overwhelmed. Fitz Lee at once rose to the occasion; it was impossible to draw in our extended lines, as a very large proportion of our men were dismounted and fighting on foot. He seized several batteries and massed them in a favorable position in the rear of our lines, facing to our rear and rallying to their support all mounted men in reach, opened upon and presented a firm front to the rapidly advancing column, the effect of which was to cause the enemy to halt, and then, taking a direction to our left, they broke away into a gallop, to our immense relief. In a few moments we found they were being pursued by Stuart, who, with Hampton's division, was driving them pell-mell before him, and what bid fair to be a great disaster was turned into a brilliant success, as our lines, relieved from this threatened danger, pressed forward with renewed determination and forced the enemy over the river. In the meantime, General Lee, with the main body of the army, continued his flanking movement and crossed the river, advancing upon Warrenton, while Meade continued his retreat to the old Manassas lines. During this movement Hill, with his corps, struck the federal line of march at Bristoe station, on the Orange & Alexandria Railroad, and attacked, without proper precaution or formation, Warren's corps of the Army of the Potomac, meeting with a severe repulse, losing several guns. This check permitted Meade to concentrate, and General Lee finding he could not bring on an action under favorable circumstances, concluded, after a rest of a day or two, to return to the Rappahannock. As soon as the backward movement commenced the enemy pushed forward their cavalry, but their enterprise soon received a decided set-back in an affair which became familiarly known as the "Buckland races." Stuart, with Hampton's division, retired slowly on the Warrenton pike, pressed by Kilpatrick, resistance being made sufficient to require the federals to proceed slowly and bring into action their heavy force. Then Stuart retreated more rapidly, and thus conveyed the impression that he was beaten, when Kilpatrick put in his entire force and pressed hard after the apparently defeated confederates. Just as the federal columns were passing Buckland, a small settlement on the turnpike, Fitz Lee, with our division, came charging in on the exposed flank of Kilpatrick, and while the latter was making preparation to meet this unexpected assault, Stuart turned and attacked in front. Under this combination the federals gave way, after a spirited resistance, and then broke into a rout, while the victorious confederates pursued them until they found refuge behind Meade's infantry lines at Gainesville. We captured a number of prisoners, ambulances, including Kilpatrick's headquarter wagons, and broke up their organization at least for that day. The service during this advance movement was most severe. During the ten days or such matter which elapsed from the crossing of the Rapidan to the return to the Rappahannock the cavalry had not more than two or three days' rations issued to them, nothing to the horses. One night we spent in a piece of oak woods near Manassas in a drenching rain, which effectually extinguished all camp fires, and for several days the little we could pick up in this desolated country during the day was supplemented by the acorns we found under the trees at night; these were split and roasted in the embers after the manner of roasting chestnuts, but they were a monstrous poor substitute. Persimmons were in reasonable abundance, but in the early days of October they had not undergone the mellowing influences of frost, which make that fruit under such circumstances fairly palatable. In addition to these privations, we were almost continually in contact with the enemy and under fire from his cavalry or infantry. It was consequently with ill-disguised satisfaction we crossed the Rappahannock, particularly as the purposes of the movement had so entirely failed to bring about anything like result.

After the return we took position near Brandy station, not far from the residence of Mr. J. Minor Botts, who enjoyed the reputation of being "all things to all men," with a decided proclivity to sympathy with the Union cause. While we lay here I received my promotion to be Captain. The appointment was handed me by Colonel Brown, who had recommended to Gen. Fitz Lee that I be promoted, which the latter had forwarded with his hearty approval, and as this was the first intimation that such was in contemplation it was to me doubly agreeable, as well as a surprise.

In November Colonel Johnson came to the front with an order from the War Department to command the Maryland Line, and General Lee directed him to assemble the various commands at Hanover Junction for the protection of the bridges over the North and South Anna rivers, near that point, and to hold and to observe the country in the direction of the peninsula, and thus protect Richmond from any movement from that quarter. The commands so assembled were the 1st Maryland Cavalry, Col. Ridgely Brown; 1st Maryland Infantry, Capt. J. Parran Crane, commanding; 1st Maryland Artillery, Capt. W. F. Dement; 2d Maryland Artillery (Baltimore Light), Capt. W. Hunter Griffin; 4th Maryland Artillery (Chesapeake), Capt. W. S. Chew—in all about 800 men.

To the above was added a fine Virginia battery, under command of Captain Cooper. The men were sheltered in huts, and the camps arranged with a view of passing the winter with the greatest comfort. The proximity to Richmond permitted us to draw on the resources of that city, as circumscribed as they were, while the neighboring village of Ashland provided a society of the fair sex which was especially grateful, consisting as it did of many who had "refugeed" and forsaken their homes as they became included in the federal lines. A log church or chapel was erected, to which the ladies of the vicinity would come and listen to the faithful ministrations of our Chaplain, the Rev. Mr. Duncan. Glee clubs were formed and frequent concerts were given, as well as other amusements, to relieve the tedium of a long winter. The infantry and artillery spent their time mostly in camp, but the cavalry had the advantage of outpost service and scouting, which made the time pass more quickly to them. From November to May the Maryland Line in this position enjoyed the association of comradeship and constituted the recognized representation of Maryland in the Army of Northern Virginia. I had been assigned to duty as Assistant Adjutant-General of the command, and in the discharge of this duty had an amount of liberty that was peculiarly grateful and agreeable to me. Capt. W. C. Nicholas was assigned as Assistant Inspector-General, Maj. G. H. Kyle as Commissary, Maj. Chas. Harding as Quartermaster, and Dr. Richard Johnson as Surgeon, with the Rev. Thomas Duncan as Chaplain. We constituted a most happy and congenial family.

About Christmas I obtained leave of absence for a few days, and spent that joyous season with dear friends in the county of Essex, on the lower Rappahannock, about fifty miles from camp.

1864.

1864.

In March intelligence was received that the enemy had started a cavalry expedition from their lines beyond the Rapidan, and having passed the flank of General Lee, were approaching the Junction. At once all was astir, the infantry was posted supporting the batteries which at once took position to defend the railroad bridges, while Colonel Johnson, with such of the cavalry as were available, at once started out to observe and follow the enemy's column, which took the direction of Richmond, not halting to attack our position at the bridges. The cavalry was scattered, reaching down the Pamunkey, in the direction of the White House, observing the lower ferries and the country toward the line of the York River Railroad, and Colonel Johnson could only get together something less than 100 men to operate against the new enemy, who proved to consist of a picked force, under Kilpatrick, and had for their object the capture of Richmond, the release of federal prisoners there confined, and, to their eternal shame, their written instructions, which fell into our hands in the course of the operations against them, contemplated the burning of that city and the killing of President Davis and his Cabinet. Kilpatrick had as his principal assistant in this expedition Col. Ulric Dahlgren, who had conceived this vile plan and was charged with its execution. From the time Colonel Johnson struck the enemy's line of march he did not lose sight of them day or night, but by constant attack, the boldness of which completely concealed the poverty of his numbers, retarded their movements and finally thwarted their schemes. At Yellow tavern we captured a party bearing dispatches from Dahlgren, who had struck out for the James above Richmond, and was approaching with his detachment from that direction Kilpatrick, who, with the main body, was then engaged with the outer defenses at Richmond. Dahlgren notified Kilpatrick in these captured dispatches of his purpose to attack, and asked that the latter co-operate. Johnson's attack on Kilpatrick's rear, however, disconcerted that officer, who was evidently under the impression he was being assailed in force, and he suspended his attack on Richmond and prepared to look after the safety of his command. General Hampton coming up with a part of his division, attacked his camp that night, capturing a number of prisoners and horses. The effect of this was to confirm Kilpatrick in his conviction that his command was in great danger, so, disregarding Dahlgren and his detachment, leaving them to work out their own salvation, as soon as it was light he retired down the peninsula, pursued by the Maryland cavalry, which had in the meantime gotten together. Dahlgren, with his command, ran the gauntlet in the effort to rejoin Kilpatrick, sustaining heavy loss in men and horses, himself being killed in an encounter with a number of home guards and cavalrymen, at home on furlough, near King and Queen Court House, his body falling into the hands of our people, and with it the condemning evidence of the infamous scheme which he had in contemplation.

The work of the Maryland cavalry in this affair won for them and Colonel Johnson most distinguished notice. They were thanked in general orders, and General Hampton in his report gave to them the credit of saving Richmond from capture. For some two months after the foregoing, things settled down again in the same quiet routine which had prevailed during the winter, until Grant, who had assumed command of the federal armies, with the grade of Lieutenant-General, commenced his forward movement by crossing the Rapidan and taking position in the Wilderness about May 3d, when ensued a series of bloody engagements, which resulted with alternate success to either side, but, by reason of his immense superiority in numbers, he was enabled to hold Lee's front and, by extending his right, finally forced the latter to retire to the old lines before Richmond. This movement also caused the breaking up of our pleasant camp at Hanover Junction and the distribution of the Maryland Line, the various organizations being assigned to their respective arms of the service. Before this was done, however, another cavalry raid was made by Sheridan with the entire cavalry force of the Army of the Potomac, with the purpose of destroying the lines of railroad in the rear of General Lee, and the capture of Richmond, if possible. As soon as the head of Sheridan's column struck the Virginia Central Railroad at Beaver Dam, a few miles north of our position at the Junction, Colonel Brown, with a portion of the 1st Maryland Cavalry, attacked them in their camps at night and made things very interesting. There was something of sublime audacity in this attack of not more than 150 men upon a body who numbered not less than 8000 of as finely-equipped and organized cavalry as had ever been brought together on this continent. Of course, when the morning light exposed the insignificance of the attacking party it did not take long to drive them off, and Brown withdrew to our defenses at the Junction, where we had again taken position to cover the bridges under our care. All day long from our position we had in view the long lines of federal cavalry as they marched by in the distance, heading toward Richmond, and momentarily expecting they would stop and pay their respects to our small command. Toward night General Stuart came up with what of his cavalry he could get together, following Sheridan, the head of whose column was now near the defenses at Richmond. Stuart's force was much reduced and he was in need of artillery, having broken down his own batteries in the rapid march he had been making to overtake Sheridan. Stopping for a few moments, he asked Colonel Johnson to lend him one of our batteries, the Baltimore Light, promising to take good care of it and to return in a few days. While not anxious to thus let out one of our best batteries, yet the occasion was so serious that no objection could reasonably be offered, and the battery accompanied Stuart, whose purpose was to attack Sheridan in the rear as he was engaged with the forces in the works at Richmond. At Yellow tavern Stuart made his attack, but his small force was unequal to the task and was overwhelmed, his lines being driven back, and for a moment our battery fell into the hands of the enemy. Stuart, rallying a small body of men, returned to the charge and rescue, and in this effort was killed. McNulty, who took command after Griffin was wounded, succeeded in the *melée* in getting off with two of his guns, leaving the remaining two in the hands of the enemy and sustaining heavy loss in men and horses. This rough handling of our favorite battery, in which we had so much pride, and which went out from us in such admirable condition for service, was particularly trying, but, above all, was the overpowering sorrow at the loss of the gallant Stuart, the Rupert of the Confederacy, whose signal abilities had been so often displayed and under whose brilliant leadership the cavalry of the Army of Northern Virginia had won such renown. In the contemplation of the reckless daring of this distinguished soldier, the jovial, rollicking character of his temperament and the audacity of his enterprise, a stranger is at loss to understand that the man himself was as quiet in his demeanor and as modest in word and thought as a blushing girl, and, like our great captains—the noble Lee and the lamented Jackson—was a devoted Christian, who illustrated in his daily work the teachings of the Christ. Altogether of a different type from them in natural character and flow of exhuberant animal spirit, proceeding from his youth, and almost faultless physique, yet in their deep piety of thought and reliance in their Redeemer, together they formed a trio of Christian excellence, examples of the beauties of that faith which they practiced with true childlike submission and obedience. Happy indeed was it for the young men of the South that in the demoralizing and degenerating influences of war as found in large armies, the promiscuous associations and of necessity the extended license and temptation to evil to which they were exposed, they had before them the lovely characters of such great and pure men, who, by the influence of their unostentatious example, served to give a savor of life and hope in the midst of death and the destructive agencies, which are so largely in the ascendancy when men's passions are aroused, and moral restraint so curbed and in subjection as in times of war. There was nothing of cant or Puritanical exclusiveness in the religious development of these men, and there existed in the Army of Northern Virginia, to a marked degree, the same deep-seated piety and reverence for things holy and divine which made its camps at times delightful seasons for those who desired to serve the Lord and do His will.

The effect of this religious influence was marked not only upon those who engaged in these frequent services, but upon others who were not professing Christians, and when, at the close of the war, the men, and more particularly the younger men, returned to their homes to begin anew a battle for life and existence, they were better men for the struggle by reason of their army religious experience, while upon all, even those not so exercised, rested the sweet influences of the purity of life and earnest devotion of Lee, Jackson and Stuart.

In the action at Beaver Dam the Maryland cavalry lost a number of officers and men, among whom was Capt. Augustus F. Schwartz, who, being wounded, fell into the hands of the enemy upon the advance of Grant a few days later. Notwithstanding his suffering and wounded condition, the federals insisted in carrying him off a prisoner, and from the effects of this journey he died shortly after reaching Washington.

General Lee retired from Spottsylvania and took position in the vicinity of Hanover Junction in the latter part of May. I remember General Early riding up to our headquarters early one bright morning. We had moved out from our cabins and winter-quarter camps, and had pitched our headquarter tents on the side of the road leading from the Junction to Taylorsville, and were still very comfortably fixed. The Colonel had a tent to himself; we had a mess tent, I had a tent for my office, and the other officers of the staff were liberally provided. We had not interpreted the order limiting tents and transportation, which General Lee had published in the spring, as being applicable to us, detached as we were from the main army. So on this particular morning our headquarters presented quite an array, with our headquarter color flying. Old Jubal rode up very leisurely, and in his usual quaint way exclaimed, "What army corps headquarters is this?" We met him most cordially, invited him to alight and tendered our hospitalities in a way that was always grateful to the old hero, when he again remarked, "I certainly thought I had struck an army corps," and added, "General Lee will be along presently and he will be very apt to say something about his order as to sending tents and baggage to the rear." I took the hint at once, and in fifteen minutes everything was down, packed and loaded, save one solitary tent, and when shortly afterwards the troops began to file by, and General Lee rode along and enquired for General Early, he was directed to the sole evidence of our former comfort and grandeur. General Lee looked very much worn and troubled. The terrible responsibilities which had been forced upon him, and the strain to which he had now been subjected for the three or four weeks past, were telling on his endurance, and, added to this, he was really a sick man. I stepped into the tent and informed General Early that General Lee wished to speak to him, and he immediately arose and went out. In a moment or two I had occasion to pass out, and in so doing overheard General Lee say, "General Early, you must not tell me these things, but when I give an order, see that it is executed," or something to that effect. I afterward learned that General Early had mentioned the wearied and weakened condition of his men, and expressed himself that they might not be physically able to perform some service General Lee desired. When we recall what these men had undergone from May 5th, when Ewell's corps struck the advance of Grant under Warren, on the old turnpike at the edge of the Wilderness country, through the succeeding days of incessant battle or march, which finally culminated at Spottsylvania Court House on May 12th, when Hancock captured a salient point on their line and with it the better part of Johnson's division; then the bull-dog tenacity with which they held on to their new lines under repeated assault and under a fire which mowed down the very trees of the forest; the sleepless nights of constant apprehension through which they passed, and then the rapid march to keep between Grant and the threatened Capital, and now, with ranks thinned by battle and worn by fatigue, they sought a moment's repose, one can well understand how their commander might be tempted to utter a word of mild remonstrance against further exactions. General Early, as he walked back to the tent and Lee rode off, remarked, "General Lee is much troubled and not well." For several days General Lee offered battle to General Grant in this position between the North and South Anna rivers, but the latter declined to lift the gage, and again resorted to his tactics of swinging around the confederate right.

While waiting in this position for General Grant's attack, General Lee sent for Colonel Johnson, and stated he was very much in need of accurate information of the enemy's movements, our cavalry being engaged in following Sheridan, and asked if he could not cross the North Anna and ascertain what the enemy was doing. Colonel Johnson took the Maryland cavalry and crossed the river below Doswell's, and, pushing out into the country, struck the Fredericksburg railroad at Penola station, when it was discovered the federals were moving in force on the telegraph road, and there was every evidence of their concentration in Lee's front. On the return we found the country through which we had passed in the earlier hours of the day was now filled with federal cavalry and our situation was precarious; in fact, we were between their infantry and cavalry lines. The only recourse was to strike across the country to the nearest point on the river and make an effort to recross. This movement was executed with great skill and at considerable risk, but fortune favored us, and the command was extricated without loss, the crossing being made by cutting down the banks of the stream and forcing our way over, not a moment too soon, as, in a little while, the enemy occupied in force. After several days spent in reconnoitering Lee's position, Grant concluded it too strong to attack, and again moved around our right. The federals crossed the Pamunkey at Hanovertown or Newton's Ferry and pressed forward to the old stamping ground of McClellan in 1862. Lee at once marched to place himself in position to cover Richmond, taking with him all of the Maryland Line except the cavalry and the two guns of the Baltimore Light Artillery. With this small command Colonel Johnson moved to Hanover Court House and then pushed down to the vicinity of Newton's Ferry to observe the enemy. Whilst near Hanover Court House I had quite an experience. We had spent the night in a piece of woods about a mile from the Court House, and in the early morning the command moved out, leaving me engaged in preparing some orders with a single courier, a little fellow from Frederick about sixteen years old, who rejoiced in the cognomen of Dixie. Dixie, or Charles Oates I believe his rightful name was, had come out with us when we were in Maryland in the previous summer, and had been detailed for service at headquarters. After finishing up my orders, we mounted and rode after the command, thinking it had gone in the direction of the Court House, but as we rode up to the tavern, what should we find confronting us but some half-dozen federal infantrymen, who also had in charge several led horses. It was a sort of "groundhog" case; they either had us or we them. Preparing at once for an encounter, and advancing rapidly, I directed Dixie to summon them to surrender, which he did in terms most emphatic, if not choice in language. They threw down their arms, and we found them to be New Jerseymen, whose brigade had just moved off, which we also proceeded to do in a reverse direction, bringing our prisoners with us. After getting them up the road some distance, Dixie asked if he could go through them. To "go through" in army parlance meant to conduct a searching examination, more particularly devoted to the taking of an accurate inventory of personal effects and belongings. I authorized Dixie to go ahead, and he relieved one of the men of a silver watch, which he asserted was especially valuable to him as the gift of a sister, and appealed to me strongly not to let the little chap despoil him in this way. I explained to him that there was little prospect of his success in holding on to his property, as when we turned him over to the provost guard it was more than likely it would be taken from him, and as

Dixie had captured him he was certainly better entitled to the plunder, and refused to interfere. As Dixie turned over the contents of their knapsacks there appeared a pair of army trousers, new and apparently never worn. These took my eye, and I offered to purchase, asking the fellow what they were worth. He said they had just been issued to him, and the government price was something like $3. This amount I turned over to him in confederate currency and in turn took the breeches. He seemed willing to the bargain, but it was really an enforced transaction; still, as in the case of the watch, there was no probability whatever that he could have retained possession of his property. On meeting with a body of W. H. F. Lee's brigade I turned our prisoners over to them, retaining the horses for our own command. In the course of the summer or early fall Dixie was unfortunate enough to be captured himself, and, by a curious coincidence, he fell into the hands of the New Jersey brigade to which these men belonged, and one of them, who had been exchanged, recognized him and he paid rather dearly for his watch. On his return, just before or after the close of the war, I forget which, he told me of his experience, and further stated they were very pointed in their enquiries for "that Captain," and intimated if they could get hands on him it would not be altogether so pleasant.

About May 27th we approached within some three miles of Mrs. Newton's and found Gordon's North Carolina cavalry brigade dismounted and engaged with the enemy in the direction of the ferry, their led horses occupying the road, which was intersected at this point by another road leading off in the direction of Jack's Shop. Colonel Johnson determined to move down this road, and well it happened for the North Carolinians that he did so, for we had not proceeded more than one-half or three-quarters of a mile before we met their picket squadron coming back in haste, reporting the enemy was closely following them. As these men rapidly rode by our little column, the firing just ahead of us down the road gave evidence that their statement was correct. We were in column in a rather narrow road, the left side of which bordered on a heavy, swampy piece of timber, while on the right was a ditch surmounted by a stout fence, beyond which were the open fields of quite a large farm. Colonel Johnson at once had the fence torn down and turned the head of the column into the field, while I rode back to the other squadrons and had them do likewise, it being important to get out of the road and effect some formation to meet the advancing enemy. The guns were unlimbered and turned around in the narrow road and sent back to the cross road where Gordon's horses were, with instructions to keep out of the way until we developed the enemy's force. Before the regiment could complete the formation in the field, we were under heavy fire, but for some twenty minutes or more held our ground, suffering considerable loss. In the meantime I had gone to our right and taken position on a hill which afforded some view of the country and which was occupied by Captain Rasin with his troop. It did not take long to comprehend the situation; we had in front of us not less than a full brigade of federal cavalry, who were now advancing on our devoted command, which was holding its position with great tenacity. Colonel Johnson, realizing the danger he was in, gave orders to withdraw, and sent me word to bring Rasin and come in, as he was going to leave. At this time the enemy made a charge in line, and their dense masses came toward us as if to swallow up the little command. Colonels Johnson and Brown moved off in good order, but in passing through an opened gateway leading into an adjoining field, by some misfortune the gate was closed, leaving the rear troop in the field with the advancing enemy. Colonel Brown, with that gallantry and devotion for his men which ever marked him, took position endeavoring to open and so hold the gate, in order that the men might escape, and while thus engaged was several times struck on the head by the sabres of the enemy, who were now among his men. The command then struck a gallop, and the retreat was made with all rapidity, the order being passed down the line to the men to scatter and take care of themselves, as there was no chance of making resistance, and by this course the pursuit would be broken. As I turned to leave my position on the right, I was struck by a ball on the left shoulder, which tore open and mutilated my jacket and nearly threw me from my horse by the force of the blow. In this I lost my hat, which fell to the ground—a new hat it was and a valuable hat to me. I had paid $170 for that hat in Richmond not many days before, and there it was on the ground, with its gilt cord and handsome black plume of which I was very proud. I could not afford to lose that hat, and yet riding rapidly toward me were some six or eight federals, whom, under the circumstances, I did not particularly care to meet. I looked at the hat and then at these people, and determined to try for it; so I dismounted, recovered my property, my horse in the meantime becoming very restless, and by the time I was again on his back they were upon me, firing rapidly from their revolvers. I was alone and saw the command down the hill to my left was retiring, so I turned and put my horse at top speed down the hill to rejoin them on their retreat through the next field. On reaching the foot of the hill I found a stiff fence on a ditch bank in the way, but there was no time to look for gates or low places, for my pursuers were not fifty yards behind me. At the fence I went like a shot and put the spurs to my horse as I held him up for the leap, and over we went in safety. On reining up in a few yards I faced about, and then had the privilege of returning the compliments which had been so freely bestowed, as I found my pursuers could not make the fence, their steeds not being equal to it. The federals followed us for perhaps a couple of miles and then gave up the pursuit. We had lost heavily in this encounter, about fifty men killed and wounded and prisoners, but we undoubtedly saved Gordon's brigade from destruction, as the enemy would have caught his horses in ten minutes' time and had his dismounted line at their mercy had we not made this fight. As it was they had time to withdraw without loss. I regret to record, however, they did not even so much as stop to enquire how we were making out, much less to come to our assistance. After the excitement of this contest cooled down I began to feel the effects of the injury I had received.

My entire shoulder was black with bruises, and for several days I had to carry my left arm in a sling. After the pursuit had ended we made our way to the main road leading toward Ashland, and on this road found Fitz Lee, with his command, resting on the roadside, and learned on enquiry they had just returned from an expedition to the James river, where they had assaulted some negro troops, who were sheltered by earthworks and who had repulsed the attack, and made good their defense. As we rode along through the command we presently struck headquarters, and General Fitz called out in a jocular manner, "This is a pretty howdy-do for the Maryland cavalry—let the Yankees run you off the face of the earth." Evidently we were not the first of our regiment to pass along, and the General had learned from them the story of our disaster. I blurted out in reply—not a very proper thing to do in the presence of my superior officer, but we were all well known by General Lee and always at home with him—"Well, General, one thing is certain, the people who have been after us were white men; we stayed long enough to find that out, anyway." With the utmost good humor he laughed heartily at the rejoinder he had provoked.

We all loved Fitz Lee, and he had a marked fondness for the Maryland boys. His bright, sunny disposition made things happy and pleasant for all who were attached to his headquarters. Fond of fun, yet there was no one who commanded more respect when on duty or whose able services were more pronounced in the field. He maintained his position by the force of his signal abilities and in no sense by reason of the name he bore or the relation he sustained to our great chief. To the last at Appomattox he was still the undaunted cavalryman, and his record during the four years of the struggle was not dimmed in the defeat of our cause, but more brightly shone forth in the civic life upon which he then entered, and at this writing the entire reunited country, north and south, voices his praises and its appreciation of his devotion, courage and manliness.

We soon gathered our command together, and found our

battery had gotten out all right. For the next few days we occupied a position between Hanover Court House and the railroad at Wickhams. The enemy, however, were active and drove us out and back to the vicinity of the railroad bridge over the South Anna, not far from Taylorsville.

In this position we were attacked on June 1st and compelled by force of numbers to retire, with little loss, save one and that in the person of Colonel Ridgely Brown, who, disregarding the injuries received a few days back at Pollard's farm, had returned to duty with the command. We had been skirmishing nearly all day, the enemy, by their superior numbers, forcing us back, until towards the close of the afternoon we had taken position slightly in advance of the railroad crossing. The firing was not heavy, but persistent, and Colonel Johnson and myself rode back beyond the railroad to select a new position to which we could retire the command if occasion required. We were on our return to the front when one of the men rode up and announced that Colonel Brown had been shot, and presently his body was carried by to the rear. We immediately galloped to the front and found the enemy making disposition for an advance which it was apparent we could not withstand with our small command. It became necessary to call in our skirmishers and retire in the direction of Ashland, which movement was made in good order, the federals closely following and pressing our rear. On reaching the vicinity of Ashland we found they had already occupied that point, and we had to move with rapidity through the outskirts of the village until we reached a point where we were in communication with our troops. Notwithstanding the pressure under which the movement was made, I sought out the house to which Colonel Brown had been carried and found him unconscious, with but a few moments of life in his body. The ball had entered his brain, inflicting a mortal wound. In deep sorrow, I took the last leave of this dear friend, and stooped to kiss his brow, now covered by his life's blood. Ridgely Brown was one of the best-rounded and perfected characters I have ever known. He was as true as steel and as gallant a soldier as ever mounted horse or drew a blade; pure in thought and lovely in disposition, he combined with his personal qualities an ability to command men that admitted of no trifling where duty or discipline was involved. Ever careful of the comforts of his men, and never exposing them unnecessarily, he won their respect and affection to a degree that there was implicit faith in his judgment, as well as unhesitating obedience accorded to his commands. He entered the service in the ranks, and through his marked force of character and natural soldierly abilities rose from one position to another, until he became the commander of the 1st Maryland Cavalry. In the discharge of the responsible duties which this important position devolved, he was ever equal to all emergencies and acquired distinction for himself and the regiment which he commanded. He was free from the ordinary vices of men, and while devout in his religious duties, was not at all ostentatious in his profession or dogmatic in his views. To me he was as kind and considerate as a brother, and the love I bore him was passing the love of women. His death was a great shock, and for weeks afterward I could not divest myself of the ever-recurring grief which would come up, as every day we missed his dear form and companionship. In the stirring times through which we were passing, new trials and new troubles were ever pressing upon our attention, but whenever the mind would go back to Ridgely Brown, there came an overpowering sense of the great personal loss we had sustained. Few men were ever so loved, none more deservedly.

While the cavalry was experiencing these hardships and constant combats, the infantry was no better favored, but with dogged persistency was contesting almost every foot of ground as the masses of Grant moved forward. At Cold Harbor on June 3d, the 2d Maryland Infantry, by their prompt and heroic action, recovered our lines which had given way under the federal assault, and driving back the advancing hosts, serving our abandoned guns with an efficiency which largely contributed to the repulse of the attacking columns. Grant's loss was fearful. His dead and wounded lay between the lines in the hot sun until they became offensive, and a truce was granted by General Lee to give them an opportunity to bury the bodies. It was here that the federals refused to move out again to the assault, and Grant was forced to suspend his attack and moved to the James, transferring his forces to the Petersburg lines, where they continued the operations of a siege until the ensuing year, when the end came, through the wasting away of the Army of Northern Virginia and its inability to further extend the attenuated lines to meet the constantly augmented forces of Grant and his relentless attacks. From the Wilderness to the crossing of the James, Grant had lost over 60,000 men—more, in fact, than General Lee had when the fighting began in the Wilderness. Grant's losses were made good, however, by reinforcements, while Lee received something less than 15,000 to repair the casualties in the Army of Northern Virginia. To make the matter more striking it may be said that every man in Lee's army disabled and put out of service one of the enemy in these few weeks. No more forcible statement can be made as to the character of the resistance or of the unrelenting steady purposes of Grant, who counted not the loss, so he made good the accomplishment of his determined effort "to fight it out on this line if it took all summer." From this time forward the process of attrition was made effective—the slow but never-ceasing grind of the larger against the smaller force; the one with almost unlimited resources behind them, the other facing the stern reality that they were the last and all. The lines of defense were extended until they lost the semblance of lines of battle, and became mere skirmish or vidette lines. Even under these circumstances they held their own and repulsed attack after attack, until April, 1865, when the extended lines were defended by less than 1000 men to the mile, Grant broke through with his heavy masses, and the end was at hand.

A few days prior to Grant's movement to the James, he started Sheridan out with about 10,000 cavalry in the direction of Charlottesville and Staunton. Hunter at that time was advancing up the Valley and had defeated the confederates at New Hope church, in which action Gen. W. E. Jones, our old commander, was killed. Hampton, who now commanded the cavalry of the Army of Northern Virginia since the death of Stuart, at once followed to intercept Sheridan, and the 1st Maryland Cavalry and the Baltimore Light Artillery accompanied his division, which reached Trevillian's station just in time to oppose the head of Sheridan's force as it attempted to cross the line of the railroad. For two days the battle raged; at one time Custer, with his brigade, broke through our line and captured the horses of Butler's brigade, the men being engaged at that time on foot. We had just reported to Rosser on our left, when the news of this mishap reached him. At once he started for the scene of difficulty, charging into Custer's column, now somewhat disordered by their success, and in a little time they were defeated and we had them on the run, recovering Butler's horses and making many captives of both men and horses from the enemy. Notwithstanding Hampton could not muster more than one-half the force of Sheridan, he held his position and repulsed every attack and forced him to give up his expedition and return to Grant's lines. I have never thought Hampton's fight at Trevillian's, the most extended cavalry engagement of the war, has ever received proper attention or appreciation.

After the battle Colonel Johnson was directed to proceed to Charlottesville with the Marylanders, while General Early, with the 2d corps, moved to Lynchburg to intercept Hunter, who was threatening that point after a march up the Valley, marked by the torch, which now was introduced as a weapon of offense in the hands of our adversaries.

Private buildings and homes, as well as institutions of learning, were sacrificed by this revengeful commander, whose early lessons in the art of hellish warfare against noncombatants, women and children were soon to be improved upon by his successors and to make the beautiful Valley of the Shenandoah a desolate waste, over which even a "crow would be compelled to carry rations." Early reached Lynchburg just in time to save it from the fate of Lexington, and Hunter was forced to retire through the mountains of southwest Virginia. We had now moved from Charlottesville and were encamped near Waynesboro, when Early asked that some information be obtained as to the location of the enemy in the lower Valley, indicating his intention of moving in that direction. As my duties as Adjutant-General were but nominal with so small a command, I offered to go below and make the scout for General Early. Taking five or six picked men, I moved off, and did not meet with any federals until near Winchester. Just as we were approaching the town, however, a body of federal cavalry came out, advancing up the turnpike. We were not sent out to fight, but to secure information, but did not care to retire before this body without exchanging a few shots, when they charged us and we had to strike out across the country until we reached the Berryville road. My experience in the lower Valley made me entirely familiar with the country, and we had no difficulty in eluding our pursuers. For several days we scouted the vicinity of Shepherdstown, Leetown and Charlestown, and located the enemy and their force, although but little information could be gained from the inhabitants, as they were completely terrorized by the excesses which had been committed by Hunter's forces, and feared every stranger, no matter what uniform he wore. In fact, the federal scouts, "Jessie Scouts," as they were termed, after the lady of General Fremont, wore the grey in order that they might work to greater advantage in this debatable ground. Among other things, I was charged with communicating with Colonel Mosby and arranging for his co-operation with Early in the proposed advance into Maryland. I found Colonel Mosby one evening after dark; he had just been down on the Baltimore & Ohio Railroad and was returning with the fruits of his expedition or raid. He at once expressed his willingness to co-operate, and in the morning I started back to report the information gained, and met General Early on the Valley turnpike about Newtown. In my absence Colonel Johnson had received his long-looked-for promotion to Brigadier-General, and had been assigned to the cavalry brigade formerly commanded by Gen. W. E. Jones. At last this long-deferred justice was granted. The former recommendations of Jackson and Ewell were supplemented by those of Hampton and the record of the brilliant service in defense of Richmond against the incursions of Kilpatrick and Sheridan, and the War Department was compelled to recognize his ability and claims. I was at once assigned to duty as Adjutant-General of the brigade. The condition of the 1st Maryland Cavalry at this time was somewhat a source of anxiety and extreme solicitude. They were deprived by the death of Colonel Brown of his careful and conservative ability. Major Smith was yet disabled from the effect of his wound received at Greenland Gap, and, in fact, was never able to resume active service in the field. Capt. F. A. Bond, the senior Captain, was wounded and a prisoner, and the next in rank, Captain Emack, was not acceptable to the officers or men, not by reason of want of gallantry, but there did not prevail that confidence in his judgment or administrative ability which would have enabled him to hold the command in a state of efficiency. So long as Colonel Johnson remained with the regiment these troubles did not become prominent, but on his assuming command of the brigade they immediately called for intervention and treatment. Colonel Johnson and myself both talked the matter over with Captain Emack, who was disposed to assert his right to succeed to the command, but we finally prevailed on him to relinquish his claims for the present and attach himself to brigade headquarters, while Capt. Warner Welsh took charge of the regiment. The brigade to which Johnson had been assigned was largely composed of troops from southwest Virginia and numbered at the time something like 1500 men, fairly mounted, but most indifferently armed and equipped. The principal arm was the long musket, which was terribly unwieldy on horseback. There was good material in the ranks and some few officers of decided merit and ability. Had it been possible to have taken them in hand earlier in the struggle and subjected them to proper training and discipline, there is no question but a most effective body could have been evolved, but now they were lacking in many of the features which were essential to successful service, particularly when it is remembered they were to be pitted against the superb cavalry of Sheridan, who was shortly sent to the Valley with the flower of his corps. In the first encounters, however, they behaved with spirit and fair steadiness, and we were, as a rule, successful. On crossing over into Maryland Johnson was sent to threaten Frederick until Early could come up with the infantry, who were greatly fatigued by reason of their long marches after Hunter, and back again down the Valley. A scheme had been devised in connection with this movement into Maryland, which had for its object the release of the confederate prisoners at Point Lookout. This plan had the sanction of the President and General Lee, and its execution was committed to General Johnson. It was dependent, however, upon Early's maintaining a position to which the prisoners could be conducted, and the subsequent rapid concentration of the federal troops for the defense of Washington destroyed the plan and necessitated his withdrawal and the calling back of Johnson, just as he was about to make his movement into southern Maryland. While we were occupying the attention of the enemy in front of Frederick, Early moved up and on his approach Johnson struck off in the direction of New Windsor and Westminster, until the line of the Northern Central Railroad was reached at Cockeysville, at which point Gilmor was detached with his battalion, the 2d Maryland Cavalry, with instruction to proceed to the Gunpowder and destroy the bridge at that point, on the Philadelphia, Wilmington & Baltimore Railroad. This movement was executed, Gilmor capturing a train near the Gunpowder upon which was Maj.-Gen. W. B. Franklin, who, however, succeeded in getting away from him while he was making his way back to the Potomac. From Cockeysville we approached through the Green Spring Valley to within a few miles of Baltimore, which was in a state of great excitement, apprehending capture. A small party under Lieutenant Blackistone, of the 1st Maryland, was sent to the country place of Governor Bradford, near Charles street avenue, with orders to burn the house in retaliation for the destruction by Hunter of Governor Letcher's house at Lexington, in the Valley, a few weeks previous. While waiting for this detachment to return we struck the establishment of Painter, the then well-known ice-cream man, about daybreak, and found his wagons loaded with this product, just about starting for the Baltimore market. It was a most ludicrous sight to see the ice cream dished out into all conceivable receptacles, and the whole brigade engaged in feasting on this, to many, a novel luxury as the column moved along. The men carried it in hats, in rubber blankets, in buckets and old tin cans—in fact, anything that would hold the cream was utilized. No spoons were at hand, but as fingers and hands were made before spoons, the natural and primary organs were brought into play. A number of the men from southwest Virginia were not familiar with this delicious food, but were not slow in becoming acquainted with its enticing properties and expressing themselves as being very much satisfied with the "frozen vittles," as they termed it. It was not the intention to do more than to threaten Baltimore, our objective point being Point Lookout. We, therefore, passed around the city, crossing the Baltimore & Ohio Railroad about Woodstock and from thence headed toward the Washington Branch at Laurel. On learning that a considerable body of infantry was at this point we passed farther on and crossed the railroad at Beltsville, six miles nearer to Washington. Near Beltsville we found a large number of government mules, some several hundred; these would serve admirably to mount some of the prisoners, and they were at once driven up and secured. We had stopped at this point to feed, and had just mounted and reformed the column and started to march on the Marlboro road, when Johnson received a message from General Early directing him to abandon the enterprise and rejoin him at once at Silver Springs, the Blair place, on the Rockville road out of Washington, and stating he would hold on for us until 9 o'clock that night. The direction of our column was at once turned, and we moved down the Washington turnpike as far as the Agricultural College, meeting on our way a body of federal cavalry, which had been sent out from Washington to investigate us. We at once attacked these people and drove them out of our way and pursued them to the very defenses of Washington. From the College we struck across the country, being fortunate in having in the Maryland cavalry a number of men from this immediate neighborhood and who were thus able to guide our march. By dark we were skirting the outer lines of earthworks around Washington, but the night concealed our movements and we were not molested. This circumstance was most favorable, as in the narrow roads our column of some 1200 or 1300 men, together with our battery the ordnance wagons and ambulances, made quite an extended line, and this was aggravated by the captured mules, which we were driving along, loose, in the road. I was directed to take the advance, and sent out men to picket and hold each intersecting road leading toward Washington, and frequently the pickets would go forward not more than a few hundred yards, before they drew the fire of the federal outposts. Had it been daylight our movement would have been impossible, as in some instances we would have been in range of the heavy guns in the defenses. It was with no little relief, therefore, when, shortly after 9 o'clock on the night of July 12th, I struck the Rockville road and reported our arrival to General Early, who was mounted and observing his infantry as they marched along the road in the retirement from the position they had occupied for the past two days in front of the Capital. After our long and arduous service we hoped, now that as we had reached the main body, to have a season of relief, but Early directed that we halt until the infantry had passed and then to protect his rear. Early the next morning we passed through Rockville and took the direction of Poolesville, the federal cavalry following very closely and at times forcing us to stop and beat them back. This, however, was not a difficult task until we reached Poolesvile, when the pressure became uncomfortable and there were indications of an attempt on their part to force an action. The brigade was halted and dispositions made to receive the attack, and a very lively combat ensued, lasting for an hour or such matter. In this affair we were victorious and succeeded in capturing a number of prisoners, driving the enemy back in confusion in a well-directed charge. In the course of this day Captain Nicholas, of the staff, behaved with marked gallantry, leading repeated charges, but was so unfortunate as to fall into the enemy's hands in one of the *mêlées*. After this affair at Poolesville we had no further trouble; the lesson which they had been taught served its purpose, and our pursuers remained at comfortable distances, although not losing sight of our rear until we recrossed the Potomac.

From a militay standpoint, Early's campaigns into Maryland had failed in its objects, which may be stated were threefold—first and principally to compel Grant to make considerable detachments from the Army of the Potomac to defend Washington from its threatened danger, and thus relieve the pressure on General Lee, which was now a matter of deep solicitude; secondly, if circumstances so turned out as to make possible, the capture of Washington itself, the effect of which would necessitate the abandonment of the operations before Richmond, with the possibility of creating an impression abroad which could be turned to our advantage. Even at this late day there still existed some hopes of recognition on the part of some of the European powers; and thirdly, and incidentally only, the Point Lookout scheme, it being hoped that if a body of our cavalry could be rapidly moved to that point, its garrison would not be able to make good the defense, occupied, as they were, with the care of 10,000 or more confederate prisoners in their charge, whom it was assumed would be recaptured and marched back through the country, seizing arms and horses and be able to make connection with Early in the vicinity of or beyond Washington.

There were several reasons why the plans fell through. In the first place, Early delayed and lost precious time before crossing into Maryland. This was doubtless due to the necessity of resting his troops, if but for a day, after their tramp after Hunter and then down the Valley, in which forced marches the men were greatly fatigued and the strength of his command somewhat impaired. Again, the resistance he encountered at Monocacy, where on July 9th he had to fight a severe battle, in which he was eminently successful, the federals sustaining an unquestioned reverse; yet this consumed valuable time and hindered his arrival before Washington and afforded opportunity for preparations to meet his attack, and, finally, the opportune arrival of the Sixth corps from the Army of the Potomac, and a portion of the Nineteenth corps from Louisiana, which had been ordered to Grant, and on arrival at Fort Monroe was diverted to Washington to assist in manning the defenses. This last circumstance was altogether unforeseen; it was one of the accidental features which become prominent in war by reason of the great results which hinge on such occurrences. These troops in themselves outnumbered Early's forces. To these should be added the regular garrison of Washington and the various guards, etc., who, under such exigency as now confronted them, were available for defense. As bearing on the number of these troops, the tri-monthly return of General Augur, who was in command, for July 10th, the day before Early appeared before Washington, shows "present for duty" 834 officers and 22,680 men; included in this total are the troops in the district of St. Mary's, which, I presume, comprehended the Point Lookout garrison and the lower Potomac country, 2132 officers and men, leaving 21,382 officers and men. These were, of course, distributed among the defenses on both sides of the river, but as the confederate operations were confined to the Maryland side the bulk of the force was free to meet Early's attack. Early's force was not more than 12,000. It will be seen at once he found himself outnumbered nearly, if not fully, three to one, and, in addition, the forces of Hunter, which he had chased away from Lynchburg, had retired through Western Virginia to the Kanawha and were now being hurried by rail to Harper's Ferry to operate on his rear. To assault so superior a force behind strong entrenchments, on which the skill and labor of the federal engineer had been devoted for nearly three years, would have been rashness approaching to folly or madness, and it became necessary to withdraw promptly. The Point Lookout enterprise was necessarily contingent on other operations. It was of doubtful success at best, and certainly under existing circumstances could not be considered for a moment.

After the return to Virginia we moved through Loudoun over the mountains and into the Valley below Winchester. The enemy followed us into Virginia, and finally took position on the Williamsport and Harper's Ferry lines.

Our cavalry were almost in daily contact with that of the enemy, and our weakness in this arm, both in character and numbers, was beginning to be unpleasantly apparent. Early kept shifting about, making the most of his small force and magnifying it by his constant activity. The federals were, however, organizing an army to crush him, and to General Sheridan was this task assigned, with a force of upwards 40,000 men, including two fine divisions of his cavalry from the Army of the Potomac.

On July 29th the brigades of McCausland and Johnson, under the command of the former, crossed the Potomac above Williamsport, about Clear Springs, and pushing out rapidly toward Greencastle and Chambersburg, reached the latter point about daylight on the 30th, General Early making a demonstration with infantry in the direction of Hagerstown. On our arrival at Chambersburg, under written orders from Early, a demand was made upon the authorities for a contribution of $100,000 in gold or $500,000 in currency, in default of payment of which within a reasonable time the town was to be burned. The order stated this severe measure was in retaliation for the excesses committed by the federals throughout the South, particularly those in the Valley of Virginia. No effort apparently being made by the authorities or the citizens to raise the money, at about 11 o'clock, the specified hour, McCausland gave the order to fire the town. The troops in the town at this time were a portion of our brigade, the 21st Virginia, under Col. W. E. Peters, a

high-minded gentleman of culture and attainments and who
for years has been occupying a chair in the faculty at the
University of Virginia. General Johnson and myself had
talked over the order, which was very repugnant in character
to both, and had been hopeful the dire alternative would not
be forced upon us. It was impossible, however, to arouse
the citizens to a realization of what was coming. Perhaps
their knowledge of the near presence of Averill, with a division of cavalry, and our apparent weak force—for the regiment of Colonel Peters only had been brought into town—
led them to think it to be an idle threat, or that we would
soon be hustled out by Averill. On my delivering the order
to Colonel Peters he hesitated for a moment, and then said:
"I would be glad if you will give my compliments to General
Johnson and ask him to relieve me of this duty; it is something so hurtful to my conscience and so utterly opposed to
my ideas of a soldier's duty that I cannot bring myself to its
execution without violence to my convictions." I felt for
this honorable man and knew General Johnson himself would
appreciate the protest, and, therefore, readily consented to
bear the message. On making report to General Johnson,
he directed me to order Colonel Peters, with his regiment,
out of town and to send for Gilmor. In a short while Harry
came dashing in with his command, and the order was given
him, coupled with the injunction that no plundering would
be permitted, but that the burning must stand as a stern act
of retributive justice, and no property was to be molested
except boots or shoes and clothing for the troops as found
in the several stores. Whether this restriction was properly
carried out I cannot say; a fearful example to the contrary
was exhibited by General McCausland himself, whom I saw
coming out of a store with an armful of books, and I remember the disgust with which General Johnson and myself remarked so grave and flagrant an impropriety. It is not in
derogation to the memory of Gilmor that I chronicle he entered upon his sad and disagreeable function with promptness and with zeal. He was not troubled with compunctions
which afflicted Colonel Peters; in fact, he was a different type

of mental and moral manhood. No more gallant and brave a trooper was there in the confederate service than Harry Gilmor, but he was a rugged character, and it required the taking off of a very considerable of the rough exterior before the brightness of the hidden diamond became apparent. In his latter years he passed under the rod of suffering and affliction, and as he approached the journey through the "valley of the dark shadow" the true and genuine characteristics of his nature shone forth, as, purified by trial, the dross was cast away and he entered into the great unknown.

The burning was systematically done; door after door was opened and fires kindled, and in a little while the heart of this thriving town was in flames. The distress of the citizens, especially of the women and children, was heartrending and exemplified the hellish nature of war. It was a sight never to be forgotten and I pray God may never be witnessed again in this fair land of ours. After a while these distresses and sorrows so appealed to the men that a number of them ceased their work of destruction and engaged with the stricken citizens in efforts to subdue the flames and to rescue property, and when in the course of the afternoon the troops were withdrawn and moved out of the town, I remained among the very last in the effort to clear the town of those who were under the influence of liquor. Some several, however, remained and fell victims to the enraged populace when our troops had retired. The horrible story of the punishment inflicted upon these unfortunate wretches who, through their own vices, became a prey to the revengeful passions of the people I will not recall. It is enough to say the whole episode is one of regretful experience and unutterable sadness.

On leaving Chambersburg the command took the direction towards McConnellsburg and thence southerly to the old national turnpike, that former great highway between the Capital and the west, until we reached the town of Hancock, being followed, not at all uncomfortably, however, by Averill, with his division of cavalry. On reaching Hancock McCausland made demand upon the citizens for a sum of money, $50,000 as I remember, on default of payment threatening the town with the same fate as Chambersburg. General Johnson and myself were being entertained at the house of a southern sympathizer when this action of McCausland was reported to him, with urgent request to intervene, as it was simply a matter of impossibility to raise the money in that little burg. Johnson was indignant, and, directing me to accompany him as a witness, sought out McCausland and told him Hancock was a Maryland town, with many southern residents, whose relatives were in the confederate army, and intimating in most direct and positive language that the Maryland men of his brigade would submit to no such violent treatment. He further reminded him of the manner in which the Chambersburg burning had been conducted, under his demoralizing influence and example, and stated the attention of the proper authorities would be brought to his conduct on our return. The angry interview was cut short by some rapid firing down the road and the report that Averill was driving in our pickets. McCausland then directed Johnson to assemble his brigade and follow him on the turnpike in the direction of Cumberland, with additional instructions to destroy the bridges and otherwise obstruct the road in our rear. This march through western Maryland along this historic highway was full of interest, and it was not at all difficult to keep the enemy at a respectable distance. As we reached Cumberland the next day we found McCausland, who was in the advance, had been skirmishing with the federal force which had assembled for the defense of that point, and had about reached the conclusion that it was too strong for us to attack. The situation now became somewhat perilous. We could not advance, and Averill was in our rear. In this emergency Gilmor was directed to find a road leading toward the river over which we could pass. He picked up a citizen, placed him on a horse, and under fear of a revolver which was largely in evidence, compelled him to pilot the column that night through this rough mountainous country, until at early dawn we struck the Potomac at a point called Old Town, near the vicinity of what is now Green Spring station, on the Baltimore & Ohio Railroad. Old Town was a small hamlet on the north side of the river, the canal running through the village. Between the canal and the river was quite a ridge, fairly well timbered, which afforded a fine position for the enemy, an Ohio regiment of infantry, which had been sent to dispute our passage. The bridge over the canal had been torn up, and we had to rebuild so as to pass over our men dismounted and assail the enemy. This movement was made with success, and the federals retired over the river, which was fordable, taking position along the railroad under cover of the slight embankment, which afforded a fair protection. The ford itself was commanded by a block house not more than 100 yards from the river and but a short distance in advance of the railroad. Into this block house two companies of the infantry were thrown, the remainder occupying the railroad as stated. In addition there was an ironclad movable battery on the railroad, with locomotive attached. We pushed the head of our column down to the ford and soon developed these preparations for the defense of the crossing. The heavy timber along the river interfered with the fire from our battery, exploding the percussion shells before they could reach the block house. After some skirmishing we succeeded in getting a section of the battery, the Baltimore Light, in a position where it could reach the ironclad on the railroad track. Then occurred some of the finest work of this character I ever witnessed. George McElwee was the gunner; his first shot struck the engine and disabled it; the next entered a porthole of the ironclad and made a wreck of that also; the third struck on the railroad bed and made things fly, when the enemy moved off in haste from their uncomfortable position. The force in the blockhouse still remained, but in a little while, in company with John McCaull, one of our headquarter couriers, I rode over the ford under a flag and summoned them to surrender. On reaching the blockhouse, Colonel Stough, the commander of the regiment, came out, and after some talk agreed to surrender his men, marching them out, some ninety odd, stacking arms and executing for them a parole.

This cleared the way, for the remainder of his valiant regiment had retired out of sight, very much to the Colonel's disgust, and he expressed himself in very strong language as to their desertion.

While all this was going on, McCausland was in the rear toward Cumberland and engaged with the advance of the enemy from that quarter. After the paroling of our prisoners they were turned loose and the line of march resumed to Springfield, some seven miles distant, where we halted for the night. The next day movement was made on New Creek, or what is now known as Keyser. As at Cumberland, we found the federals here in force and well protected by defensive works, and after feeling their position, McCausland determined it unwise to order an assault, so we retraced our steps to Springfield and took the direction of Romney, continuing the march to within a few miles of Moorefield, where, on the afternoon of August 6th, we halted as we supposed for some days' rest. During these operations the intercourse and communication between Generals McCausland and Johnson was confined to that only of official duty. Johnson was directed to encamp his brigade on the near side of the south fork of the Potomac, which was quite a considerable stream at this point, while McCausland crossed over with his brigade and bivouacked on the Moorefield side of the river. The brigade was scattered in the surrounding fields. We had no tents or other shelter for the men, but along the fences they stretched their blankets and made themselves comfortable, while the horses were unsaddled and fed. We established brigade headquarters at a house on the roadside, the residence of Mr. McNeill. The battery was parked in a field just across the road, some 150 yards in rear of an apple orchard, which was immediately opposite the house. A load of corn was hauled in and emptied on the ground very near the battery. Pickets were, of course, established, and all looked forward to a rest from the fatigues of the preceding ten days. Towards evening I rode to Moorefield and beyond, to the house of Mr. Van Meter, where I had been so hospitably entertained and nursed when wounded in the spring of

1863, and paid my respects to this kind family, remaining until after supper, when I returned to the command about 11 o'clock. I found all quiet. General Johnson had retired in the house; so after unsaddling my horse in the orchard and having him fed, I turned in on the porch for a night's rest. About midnight a courier from McCausland rode up with information that at sundown Averill was reported in Romney, some twenty miles off. Nothing more definite was conveyed, but he directed that we be prepared to move early in the morning and that a scouting party be sent out beyond our picket line on the Romney road. At once an officer and twenty men were dispatched, with instructions to pass through our pickets and observe the approaches. At the same time orders were sent to the battery to have the horses harnessed and to the various regiments to saddle up. I then retired again and was soon fast asleep, from which I was awakened just about the dawn of day by the noise and commotion in the house and all around. The ladies in the house were crying, "The Yankees are here!" Jumping up at once and seizing my saddle and arms, I made my way from the porch and into the road, which was now filled with our men riding for life and crying as they passed, "The Yankees are coming!" The sharp firing going on gave evidence of this as well. Hurriedly crossing the road and jumping the fence into the orchard where our horses were picketed, I found my colored boy standing by my horse. Throwing him the saddle, I said: "Quick, Sam, saddle up," but before this could be done the federals were in the orchard, and one of them rode toward me, making a cut with his sabre, when, without time to think, I turned, leaving Sam and my horse, and ran into the field toward the battery. As I emerged from the orchard the federal column was charging by up the road not more than fifty or sixty yards distant, and being in full view I became a target for their revolvers. My only thought at this time was to escape this fire, and into a small clump of elder bushes, which happened to be in the field before me, I ran and dropped. For five mortal hours or more, sheltered by these friendly bushes, I lay in full view of the occurrences around me. From the fact that the charging column did not come back I assumed they had broken us up, and the large number of prisoners who were being brought back was additional evidence of the disaster which had overtaken us. I saw them haul away McNulty's guns, and at one time they formed quite a body in the field so close to me that, had there been a few more files, their line would have extended into the clump of bushes in which I was secreted. The McNeill house was converted into a hospital, and I could hear the conversation going on about the house, although the orchard intervened and did not permit me to see very much in that direction. I had not been long in the bush before I had a companion, the brigade Quartermaster, who came bounding out of the orchard like an old hare just started from her bed, and sought the shelter here afforded. I did not expect much in the way of assistance from this reinforcement, but, under the circumstances, I would have been glad to have the company of even a dog. Of course, during the hours we were in this hiding there was ample time to think over the situation. I felt greatly concerned for General Johnson, not seeing him at all after the alarm, and concluded he had been caught in the house. It appears, however, he must have gotten out about the same time I was aroused, and an officer of Gilmor's dismounted voluntarily and gave him his horse, being captured himself. The General at once rode to the 21st Virginia Regiment, which was somewhat to our rear, and was then making an effort to form, and endeavored to make a charge to stem the advancing enemy, but it was impossible to get the men to follow to any considerable extent, and they were all swept back to the river and across, hotly pursued, McCausland's command faring little or no better than our own in the general rout which ensued.

At first I had little idea of being able to evade capture. I carried a small leather portfolio, suspended from a strap around my shoulders, in which were the brigade papers, orders, etc. Among these documents was the order of Early for the burning of Chambersburg. This I took out and very carefully tore into the most minute particles, not caring for it to fall into the hands of the enemy. I then bethought me that Averill was the classmate of several of my friends, who had frequently spoken of him to me or in my presence, and I determined to ask to be carried to him direct, in hopes of better treatment than is usually accorded the unfortunate prisoner. As the hours wore away, however, I began to see some faint glimmering chance of escaping capture, and determined to strike out hard for the chance. The main body of the federals had passed on over the river. Apparently there was no organized body about, save the attendants at the hospital, but the corn pile, where the battery had been encamped, was a source of great tribulation to me. It was in the same open field with myself and not more than 150 yards off, and it appeared to me every cussed straggler would stop at this corn pile and feed his horse. "All things come to him who waits," however, and at last the corn pile was deserted, and I took observation all around and failed to find any mounted men in sight. I discovered, however, what was a Godsend, the adjoining field was in corn, dense in growth, now out in tassel, eight to ten feet high and not more than 300 yards away. Once within its shelter we would be free from notice. I told my companion of my plan, that at the word we would make a run for the desired haven. He demurred somewhat at the risk, but I told him he would be left to his fate if he did not follow, and at a favorable moment, when things had quieted down in the orchard and at the house, I said, "Go." How long it took us to cover those few hundred yards, and how we managed to tumble over the high post and rail fence which surrounded the corn, I cannot say, but we stopped not until we were in the recesses of the growing corn, hidden from all view, when down we dropped until we could regain breath and ascertain if our movement had been observed. It soon became evident we had not been detected, and for the first time I now thought we had even chances of getting away. We followed the corn field until we struck the river, when, to our disappointment, we found on the opposite side a number of the enemy watering their horses and lounging about. We then followed the stream for perhaps a mile or more until we struck a point where a number of huge rocks rose out of the waters, offering a favorable place to make the crossing. On the opposite side the mountains extended nearly to the water, with a road intervening. No one was in sight, and, by hook or by crook, in some way we managed to get over and at once took to the hills. It was now about 1 o'clock, and there came up a most violent thunderstorm, the rain coming down in torrents. Very fortunate for us was it we had made good our crossing, as in a little while the waters in the river submerged the friendly rocks which aided us in getting over, but we were soaked through, and with our boots full of water, our progress climbing the mountain side was very difficult and slow. Added to this was the discomfort proceeding from the intense heat, and when we finally had reached an elevation from which we could overlook the valley below we were in a complete state of exhaustion and laid down and slept for about an hour. After being somewhat refreshed by this rest we continued following a mountain path, which brought us out on a main road, and from the evidence found in the marks of horseshoes in the roadway it was apparent a large body of cavalry had passed since the rain. Whether friend or foe we could not tell, but concluded to risk the road, which we followed for some distance, until we met a small party of men, not in uniform, but who were armed. Whether they were southerners in sympathy, or union men or bushwhackers, we could not determine, but, making a display of our arms, and putting on a bold front, we met them and engaged in conversation, and soon learned they were not of our persuasion. They did not offer to molest us, however, but gave us the information that several hundred federal cavalry had not long since passed up the road in pursuit of our demoralized and retreating command. After parting company we continued on up the road, keeping a sharp lookout, until we were brought up standing by the command "halt," enforced by several guns bearing upon us from the bushes alongside the road. From this newly-threatened danger there was no escape, and we were oppressed by the conviction that all our efforts to get away had come to naught, but, to our great relief, found this party to consist of mountaineers who were hunting straggling federals and were our friends. Upon explaining our status and necessities, they kindly offered to take us to a place of safety, and conducted us to a cabin in the recesses of the mountain, where we found a night's rest and protection. We were simply beaten out with the fatigues of the day, footsore and weary. In this humble shelter we recuperated our worn bodies during the night and the next day. Then we began to devise the ways and means to resume our journey. Whilst we lay in the bushes near the McNeill house, and I was engaged in destroying public papers, my Quartermaster friend produced some of his documents and quite a large amount of confederate currency, which he said he had best make way with in the same manner, so as to prevent it falling into the hands of the enemy, as this appeared with so much certainty to be our fate. I objected to this, however, and said to him there was still a possibility of our escape, very remote indeed, but that I had not altogether lost hope, and his money, the "sinews of war," might be useful to us. The question of his accounts with the government did not enter much into the consideration, and to this day I do not know how he squared up, but this money came into play in a way that was particularly helpful. We wanted horses to get us out of the country, the price was no object, and our host thought he could meet our requirements. So off he went, and the second day turned up with two steeds, Rosinantes, of the Quixotic type, but as we were not disposed to be captious or exacting, it did not take long to transfer the titles, and, mounting our newly-mounted beasts, and receiving instructions how to avoid the highways, we set out for a more favorable locality. For several days we followed the devious mountain by-ways, until we reached the main Valley, and learning the remnants of the command were encamped at General Meems' farm, near Mount Jackson, made our way to that point. General Johnson had given out all hopes of my escape and was convinced I had fallen into the hands of the enemy, and it was with great joy and pleasant surprise that we were welcomed to headquarters. Then followed the narrative of our several experiences, and we began to get into the facts of the disastrous occurrences which had befallen the command. They were a combination of most peculiar and unlooked-for circumstances. It turned out that the scouting party which I had sent out at midnight had passed through our pickets and by some means, to this day not very clear, they were captured to a man and without the firing of a shot or the giving of any alarm. It is thought they met up with the advance of Averill, composed of the "Jessie Scouts," who wore the grey uniforms of the confederates, and had permitted themselves to fall into their hands, doubtless taking them for some of our "irregulars," who operated in this section. Upon being carried to General Averill he appreciated the advantage and pushed on to the picket post, who, in like confidence, allowed his advance to approach, under the impression they were the returning scouting party, which had but a short time previously passed out. With like fatality the picket guard was captured without any alarm being made, and after questioning some of the men, together with information given by some of the unfriendly citizens, he became convinced the way was clear for a surprise, when, throwing aside the caution and timidity which had hitherto characterized his movements, he now put everything in rapid motion, and in a short while struck our bivouacs and was soon engaged in riding down our men, who were so rudely aroused from their slumbers by the not over-polite salutations of their foes. Averill had the good sense and judgment not to waste much time on the scattered encampments first struck by him, but, forming his column, he advanced at a trot, pushing through our sadly broken up brigade, crossed the river and engaged McCausland before the latter was in any condition to make resistance, and by his bold dash he soon had the entire body on the go in a most complete rout and state of demoralization. He captured some 200 men and horses from each brigade, the losses being divided about evenly, our wagons and ambulances and the two guns of the Baltimore Light Artillery. He met with no resistance worthy of mention, and continued the pursuit until it became apparent our flying men had gone beyond his reach, when he called off the pursuit and doubtless congratulated himself upon the easy and unexpected success he had obtained. This sad affair, as was natural, provoked bitter criticism. General Early reports it had a most damaging effect upon the efficiency of his cavalry for the remainder of the campaign, and General Lee directed him to remove General Johnson if the latter was at fault. Johnson made a full report of the occurrences on the expedition, and demanded a court of enquiry to determine and fix the responsibility. There was never, in my mind, any doubt on this point, although I cannot be regarded as other than a somewhat partial witness. McCausland's management and conduct, from the time we reached Chambersburg until the fateful day at Moorefield, was destructive of discipline, without ordinary precaution and care, and found a fitting sequel in the disaster which overtook his command. Unfortunately the innocent suffered, the reputations of others were called into question, and the cause sustained a serious loss in *morale* and in material from which this particular body of troops never entirely recovered. The hope of converting them into more efficient soldiers disappeared, and we were fearfully handicapped for the remainder of the campaign. From my own knowledge I can assert that General Early was satisfied the blame for this misfortune did not lie with General Johnson. Although frequently importuned, he refused to order the court, and the fact that Johnson was kept in command for some three months would indicate that he was satisfied with his statement. The subsequent intimacy and friendship which existed between these two is also evidence that Johnson had not suffered in the estimation of his commanding officer, however much he had to bear disparagement from others, who were not familiar with the facts which a court of enquiry only could bring to light. General Early in explanation said the good of the service did not require and rather militated against this procedure.

It had in these days become manifest that the character of

the confederate trooper was not being maintained and had depreciated from the proud position occupied in the first two years of the war. Not that there were lacking instances of heroism and the most gallant bearing, but the efficiency of the cavalry arm had deteriorated since the death of Stuart. This I attribute to the mistaken policy of the government in not protecting and fostering this branch of the service. As the war dragged along many who tired of the infantry service, and had the conception that to have a good time it was only necessary to "jine the cavalry," obtained transfer, and in most cases they were a most undesirable class of men. Again, those who were forced by pressure of public opinion to go into the army, when they had exhausted all previous means of evading service, if they could furnish a horse went to the cavalry, and it became painfully apparent the average character of the accessions so received was much below that of the early and orignal volunteer. The confederate trooper furnished his own horse, and had, to a great degree, to look after his own equipments. As a rule, general officers in command did not husband their cavalry; in fact, the average infantry officer regarded it as somewhat of a nuisance. Old Jubal in particular was almost entirely disregardful of their interest and indifferent as to their care. It was a continuous case of use and abuse, until finally, when he stood most in need, he realized the lack of proper consideration had deprived him of a most necessary adjunct, as before the efficient, well-organized and equipped cavalry of Sheridan his misfortunes came upon him thick and fast. The policy in the federal army was just the reverse. Their cavalry at the outset was inferior in character, and it was soon recognized that to perfect and elevate this branch of the service was essential to success. The cavalry corps of the Army of the Potomac became as fine a body of troops as the world ever saw. They were not the refuge for the faint-hearted and the inefficient, but a transfer from the infantry to the cavalry was held as a reward of merit, a recognition for good and gallant service. It takes a stronger and better man, as a rule, to make a first-class cavalryman than it does for the infantry. One's individuality, resourcefulness and capacity is more frequently brought into play, and the strain on the courage and moral attributes of the man is more continuous. With all its imperfections, and under all its disadvantages and hindrances, it is to be said of the confederate cavalry that in the last days of the Army of Northern Virginia its star shone with the brightness of the earlier days, and from Petersburg to Appomattox it maintained its honor in a serious of glorious contests, which were the more brilliant by reason of the discouraging circumstances which surrounded their gallant behavior and steadfastness to duty. While the cause was failing and all around were the evidences of disintegration they responded to the bugle call and the charge with the vim and dash that attends success and victory, and with readiness sacrificed themselves to protect their unfortunate infantry and artillery comrades, and when the final scenes were being enacted, and the banner of the Confederacy was being furled, they rode forth in a charge that carried them beyond the lines of the surrender, and left them free to still maintain the struggle if events would justify.

I lost at Moorefield two horses, but fortunately my best and most valuable horse had been sent to the rear to recruit before we started on this ill-starred expedition. The steed purchased in the mountains had served its purpose, and on arrival at headquarters at Meem's was turned out to graze and could not be found again. He was of so little value, however, as not to occasion any heart-burning on account of his disappearance; in fact, I did not take the trouble to make any serious search for the animal at all.

While the campaign of Early into Maryland had failed in its immediate objects, it had disarranged and delayed Grant's movements in front of Richmond and Petersburg, and in order to prevent a repetition on the part of the confederates, the federal forces in the lower Valley were concentrated and materially strengthened and the command given to Gen. Philip H. Sheridan, a trusted favorite of Grant's, with instructions to press the enemy and "follow him to the death." Two divisions of cavalry from the Army of the Potomac, Merritt's and Wilson's, were also sent to the Valley, and by September 10th a force of some 45,000, according to Sheridan's full return of that date, was collected to oppose Early with his small command, which had received no considerable accessions, save the infantry division of Kershaw, probably 4000 strong, and Fitz Lee's division of cavalry, not over 1500 sabres. There were frequent encounters with the enemy, who developed considerable enterprise, but the results were not of marked character, Early occupying Winchester, with occasional trips to the lines of the railroad in the vicinity of Martinsburg. Sheridan finally concentrated beyond the Opequon, near Berryville. On September 19th, 1864, the military situation was about as follows: Sheridan at Berryville, Early scattered between Winchester and Bunker hill, on the Martinsburg turnpike, having just made one of his excursions to the railroad for the purpose, as he termed it, of "bothering the enemy and causing them to wonder what he was about." Kershaw's division had been withdrawn and had crossed the Blue Ridge into the Piedmont country, east of the mountains, in order to be nearer General Lee. At Winchester was Ramseur, with his division of about 2500 muskets, occupying a position on the Berryville road, a few miles out of town, with a small brigade of North Carolinians, under Gen. Robert D. Johnston, on outpost, guarding the approaches from the Opequon. Bradley T. Johnson's cavalry brigade, about 1000 strong, supported Johnston's infantry, with their pickets and videttes thrown out to the Opequon, but the regiments of the brigade necessarily were somewhat scattered around Winchester, wherever grass could be found for their horses, no grain or dry forage being obtainable. Rodes, with his division, was near Stephenson's depot, about seven miles below Winchester, while Gordon's division and Breckinridge's small command were still further down the road toward Bunker hill. The total of Early's force, conservatively stated, did not aggregate over 8500 or 9000 muskets, with perhaps 3500 cavalry. The cavalry of Sheridan alone very nearly, if not quite, equalled Early's infantry, while in addition he had a body of efficient infantry of over 30,000 muskets, attended by a proper complement of artillery. About daybreak on the morning of the 19th our pickets on the Opequon were driven in, and they reported the enemy advancing in force. At this time the several regiments of the brigade were scattered, grazing their horses within a radius of two or three miles; the nearest regiment was speedily summoned, and General Johnson, at a trot, went to the support of our outposts, which, under Robert Johnston, were by this time engaged with the advancing enemy. He reached Johnston not a moment too soon, as his small command, while fully occupied in their front, had been flanked by a considerable body of federal cavalry, who were charging on their rear, when Bradley Johnson turned on them with the 8th Virginia and drove them back, capturing some thirty or forty prisoners. I had been left on the main road to await the arrival of our remaining regiments and direct their movements, and in the course of thirty minutes we had effected a formation, which protected the withdrawal to Ramseur's line, where he had formed with his division. Until 9 o'clock this gallant division withstood Sheridan's advance, until the pressure became so intense as to cause its retirement, not in confusion, but the steady and persistent advance of the federal infantry permitted no opportunity for a rally or the taking up of new lines, and apparently there was nothing in the way of assistance between its position and Winchester itself. At this juncture General Johnson gathered our small brigade and in columns of fours dashed through Ramseur's retreating lines to the very front of the pursuing federal line of battle, which halted and then retired, giving him the much-needed opportunity to reform and take a long breath in a new position. The unhesitating manner in which this movement was made, together with the yells of our men as they dashed forward, encouraged by our retreating infantry, who appreciated the gallantry of the action, and the clouds of dust which arose along the road from a charge in column of 600 or 800 men, appealed so strongly to the apprehensions of the enemy that the effect most successfully accomplished the object and our loss was fortunately slight;

the very boldness of the movement saved us from destruction. As Ramseur re-established his lines we extended his flanks with our regiments, presenting as firm and imposing a front as our slender numbers would admit. About 10 o'clock General Early, with several staff officers, rode up in a body of woods, where I had just posted a line of videttes to watch the enemy, who were giving every indication of resuming the advance in force. I very forcibly presented to him the situation, and further added the federal skirmishers would move us out in a few minutes. He replied, "We will let our skirmishers go at them," and just then our line came through the woods, and pressing forward, in a few moments engaged the advancing enemy, forcing back, not only their skirmishers, but their supporting line of battle. We then began to breathe freer for a while. From daybreak until 10 o'clock Ramseur's infantry division and Johnson's cavalry brigade had withstood the federal advance, and now Rodes, and presently Gordon, with their small, but gallant divisions, had come to our assistance. The respite was but brief, however, the federals shortly resuming the attack, and this time in still heavier force. Rodes and Gordon stoutly contested this advance, and for some time successfully resisted the enemy, and in fact drove the federals back some distance, but were finally forced to give way before overwhelming numbers. General Rodes was killed in this action, and his troops were somewhat disordered by his fall; the lines were reformed, however, very near to Winchester, while Breckinridge's division, which had now also come up, took position on our left, almost at right angles to the Martinsburg turnpike. In this new and last position Early maintained himself until about 4 o'clock in the afternoon, and we were hopeful we could make good our defense until the friendly shades of night would come to our relief. To this time, although our losses had been heavy, we had kept a firm front and the enemy in check, inflicting upon them serious damage. They had achieved no special advantage, save that of forcing our more advanced lines of the early morning. Sheridan now moved his superb cavalry around to our left, and in the closing hours of the afternoon came forward in splendid array from the direction of Stephenson's depot, advancing along both sides of the turnpike in all conceivable formation, steadily moving forward, until within striking distance of Breckinridge's lines, when, with a charge, the attack was made, overwhelming, and riding over our infantry at this point, and rolling up our lines until a contagion seemed to pervade the whole army, as they gave way under the combined influence of the renewed infantry attack on their front and this cavalry charge on their flank and rear. In a little while all semblance of order and organization was lost and our infantry was retreating through Winchester, the advancing federal lines delivering their volleys, and their batteries hurling their missiles into the flying confederates. This is the first time I had ever seen our troops retire in disorder from a field of battle, and it was with a sad heart I rode to an eminence just outside of Winchester and viewed the scene. I had been sent off on some duty and was away from our brigade when the crash came. I could see far over on our right, however, an organized body of cavalry, who were apparently retiring in fair order; this proved to be our brigade, which General Johnson had succeeded in extricating from the wreck. What caused me great wonderment was the inertness of the federal pursuit. Their cavalry evidently considered they had won glory enough for one day, for they did not resume the offensive, and their infantry was contented with advancing to the town and then halting, while their batteries would now and then give a feeble shot or two in our direction. And this all in an open country, in full view of our disordered retreat and the fact that our wagon train and artillery taking the main turnpike had been arrested by the breaking down of a bridge a mile south of the town. While the bridge was being relaid our trains had no protection, save that of several batteries, which went in position because they could go nowhere else, and a few hundred of infantrymen and some stragglers, who rallied behind the stone walls. An advance on the part of a couple of regiments of cavalry or a brigade of infantry would have cleared all these away and our wagons and guns would of necessity have fallen into the hands of the enemy. Finally, however, the repairs to the bridge were made and we moved off unmolested, continuing the retreat to Strasburg, where the next day position was taken at Fisher's hill, the infantry on our right in a very strong position, while the cavalry was thrown to the left, to occupy the country to the North Mountain range, a few miles off.

Sheridan moved up and deployed in front of the Fisher's hill position, and skirmishing was pretty lively all throughout the 21st. Our cavalry lines were very much extended and thinly held, with no defenses save the protection of occasional piles of fence rails or some such shelter. The men were dismounted and the horses sent to the rear, almost a half-mile or more. This was the situation on the afternoon of the 22d, when we discovered on the slopes of the mountains on our extreme left a line of infantry making their way around our flank, the sunlight flashing on their burnished muskets and bayonets making a glimmering sheen of silver as seen through the openings in the mountain foliage. General Johnson directed me to call the attention of General Lomax to the movement, and when I found him the firing had broken out fiercely on our left and our lines were being driven back. The danger to our led horses at once occurred to me, and at a gallop I rode to the point where they were being held, one man caring for six or eight horses, so anxious had we been to strengthen our line of battle. On the way I met Lieutenant-Colonel Dorsey, with the Maryland cavalry, who was retiring before a body of the enemy, but he immediately halted at my earnest request and held the road, while I was engaged in moving the horses out of the field. The difficulty in handling so large a number of animals amid the excitement and confusion was great, but they finally were put in motion, and all would have gone well had it not been for the break in our lines at this time, which caused our men to give way in a semi-panic, and this started the men leading the horses into a gallop, and soon the whole outfit was in a helpless state of rout; saddles were slipping and turning, horses were breaking away from their holders, baggage and bundles were being spilled all along the road in the utter confusion. It was not within the limit of human ability to stop or stem the mad flying column until we reached the town of Woodstock, where I called on the provost guard to turn back or stop the flight by firing upon the runaways if necessary. By night, with the assistance of Lieutenant Chapman, I had succeeded in getting together some several hundred men, with as many more horses, perhaps, and being entirely without information as to what had transpired at Fisher's hill, started with them for the front, following the main turnpike. We had not proceeded more than a mile or two when a rumbling sound down the pike indicated a heavy movement in our direction, and it was evident an uneasy feeling had taken possession of our improvised command. We tried to steady them, but as the sound came nearer and nearer they hesitated, then turned and back to Woodstock they went at no slow pace. Patience as well as physical endurance by this time was exhausted, and Chapman and myself concluded to let our followers go to the devil if they wished, at least for this time, and we continued on our way, soon meeting with the cause of the disturbance, to wit, the army wagon train. The road being much impeded by the wagons, we determined to turn aside for a while, and so dismounted and stretched our weary bodies on the ground, holding our horses by the bridle rein, and soon fell fast asleep. We must have slept for several hours, for, when we awoke, on consulting my watch, it indicated the hour to be near about 1 o'clock. The moon was shining brightly, lighting up the turnpike and the surroundings almost as if it were day. No one was to be seen, not a sound was heard; the stillness and the lonesomeness was oppressive. Somehow I felt instinctively that things had gone wrong and we were out of place, and we, therefore, mounted our tired horses and wended our way back toward Woodstock. As we approached the town we were halted by a vidette, who allowed us to come in and report ourselves, when he said, "Well, it is likely you are the last out." We soon learned that Early's entire force had given way in the disgraceful panic, which to that time we thought had affected only our extreme left, but it turned out the infantry had behaved just as badly as our wretched cavalry and without the same justification, for the enemy had not so seriously attacked their strong lines. As the wagons were going by us on the pike I recalled they were accompanied by a large proportion of men, more than the usual wagon guard or followers, but it never for a moment suggested itself that it was the army in complete disorder that was passing.

I have never understood the occasion or cause of the break at Fisher's hill. The turning of our flank by a heavy body of infantry, supported by a strong cavalry advance, explains why our attenuated cavalry line should give way at that point, but how the whole division became involved, or why our infantry in their strong position should become panic-stricken, I do not to this day comprehend. It was one of those experiences, I suppose, which the best of troops undergo at times, the result of the worn-out condition, mental, moral as well as physical, resulting from the unremitting stress under which they had labored from May 2d, when they marched to meet Grant in the Wilderness; from that day it was constant march or exposure to battle. It doubtless was the result of the constant dripping which wears away even the stone, and human endurance gave way in a state of moral and physical collapse. Of course, there was at this time beginning to be manifested a conviction of the hopelessness of our struggle against the superior numbers and resources which confronted us. This may have been a factor, but only to a limited degree, for in a few days the infantry pulled themselves together and their good conduct was apparent in succeeding contests. The reverse at Winchester was the cause of sorrow to us, but that at Fisher's hill was felt to be disgraceful. Our loss was heavy, particularly in artillery. Sheridan claimed twenty pieces at Fisher's hill alone and 1100 prisoners. I doubt the latter greatly; our people got out of the way with such rapidity as to escape capture to the extent claimed. On the other hand, the federal official returns show Sheridan's losses in this campaign, that is, from Winchester to Cedar Creek, to have been in killed, wounded and prisoners 16,952. This statement shows the measure of resistance that was offered by Early with his small command, which at no time during these operations equaled the number of their foes they put out of service, as admitted by the returns in question. The retreat from Fisher's hill did not stop until Mt. Jackson was reached, when things again assumed shape, but Sheridan pressing forward, Early was obliged to retire in the direction of Waynesboro, leaving the way open to Staunton, which was occupied by Sheridan's cavalry.

Sheridan was now convinced that Early had been so crippled in the recent engagements as to prevent his again resuming the offensive in the near future, and as the forces taken from Grant were needed in the operations before Petersburg, determined to return to the lower Valley, executing Grant's order, however, to make the country a barren waste. We now were to experience an organized effort to destroy and burn mills, barns, crops, stock and everything that could give succor to life and being. Grant's order read, desolate the country so that "a crow in passing over must needs carry rations." We had had a foretaste of these troubles when the malignity of Milroy, of Pope and later on of Hunter, like sporadic instances of fiendishness, appeared on the scene of war. These specially offensive specimens of military hostility had excited attention and brought down on their perpetrators the condemnation of a virtuous people both north and south. But now, under the direct instruction of the commander of all the armies of the United States, was his chosen and apt lieutenant in such infamous procedure to deliberately scourge this beautiful section of our country and reduce its inhabitants to the direst poverty and want. War is not play—war is cruel—but war need not be the "hell" in the sense that Grant, Sheridan and Sherman were now about to illustrate. I have viewed from my horse the smoking fires of twenty-seven farmhouses or mills within a radius of five miles. The stock were driven off or killed, the implements of agriculture were wantonly destroyed and burned, and all that was left the ruined people was perhaps the roof over their heads and whatever of food supplies they could secrete and hide from the insatiable destroyers. The military necessity which urged this desolation, was the making of a desert of a section, through which the enterprise of the confederates threatened the country north of the Potomac and Washington, in spite of overwhelming forces arrayed in its defense. There are many traits in the character of General Grant the confederate soldier respects; the courtesy and magnanimity as displayed toward their loved Lee when the end came at Appomattox, and when the hand of disease and suffering took hold of him, the strong man now laid low, appealed to the sympathetic nature of those whose dearest objects in life had been defeated by his leadership. But there are some things we cannot and do not forget, and among these may be classed the desolation of the Valley, the brutal lust and wantonness which marked Sherman's march to the sea and the indignities which were heaped upon Mr. Davis at Fort Monroe. Time is a great physician, and after the lapse of more than a third of a century many a wound then received has healed and many an indignity has been forgiven; but while we are human and life lasts—nay, while the world has a conscience and detests unnecessary cruelty and crime—these diabolical deeds, perpetrated under the guise of military necessity and with fiendish delight, will ever be reprehended and the promoters held up to the detestation and scorn of the good and true, not only of our own, but of all generations to come.

Old Jubal was not so passive, however, as Sheridan imagined. As was said of him by one of the federal commanders, "This stern old soldier never knew when to stop fighting," and, as Sheridan retired, he gathered up his depleted command and followed with a tenacity and persistency that was as unexpected as it was bold and heroic.

As usual, our cavalry, which General Early denounced as being insufficient and unable to contend with that of the enemy, was kept close at the heels of Sheridan's retiring column. We had now been joined by Rosser, with his old brigade, the "Laurel brigade," as he termed it. Rosser had been made a Major-General, deservedly so, for he was one of the bravest and most enterprising of our cavalry commanders, given albeit to perhaps an undue amount of boasting, owing to a superabundance of self-esteem, but withal a soldier of considerable merit. The absence of the larger portion of the cavalry corps of the Army of the Potomac from the lines in front of Richmond and Petersburg had placed our confederate cavalry in that quarter under Hampton more on a parity with the enemy, as far as numbers were concerned, and consequently considerable success attended their operations. We called on Rosser at the Willow Pump one evening, and he very jocularly enquired why we had been permitting the federal cavalry to misuse us so terribly, stating on the Petersburg lines our people were virtually having their own way, and he would now show us how it ought to be done. I recall a very pertinent reminder that came before us that night. When Gates, fresh from the laurels which fell upon him at Saratoga, whether deservedly so or not is not the question, was on his way to his southern assignment, he lauded his past successes and predicted just as confidently his future glories, but was warned to beware else his "northern laurel" might be transformed into the "southern willow." On our way back General Johnson and myself referred to the incident as being applicable to the case in point. My dear friend, the Rev. Dr. Dame, tells this story in connection: Old Jubal's attention was attracted by the green sprigs worn in the hats of Rosser's men, and in his quaint way enquired what was the signification. "Why, General," said some one in explanation, "don't you know they call their command the 'Laurel brigade,' and these are sprigs of laurel." "I never knew the laurel was a running plant," replied old Early; "I think a pumpkin vine would be more appropriate." However, we were soon to have another exemplification of the wisdom of the admonition, "Let not him boast that putteth on the armor." On October 8th the army had advanced down the Valley as far as Newmarket, where Early halted the infantry, but pushed his cavalry to the front some twenty-five or more miles from any support, Rosser, with the brigades of Wickham, Paine and his own on the back road; Lomax, with Johnson's and Jackson's brigades, on the turnpike. At this time these two last commands did not aggregate more than 1000 or 1200 men at the outside. Sheridan had placed his infantry in camp about Tom's brook, and his cavalry in front was driven in on the infantry lines towards night, losing prisoners and some little material. We halted for the night just about two and one-half miles south of Woodstock and near Maurertown. Lomax came over to our headquarters about 9 o'clock and held a consultation with Johnson as to the movements of the morrow. Rosser sent over to advise he had driven the enemy before him and would advance again at early dawn. Lomax stated Early's orders were to keep on. He evidently was not assured as to the situation, and after he left General Johnson asked my views. I told him, perhaps with more emphasis than was becoming one of my years and rank, that if I were in command I would not wait until morning, but would move the division back to Woodstock that night, as I was satisfied the enemy had only been tolling us on during the day. One thing was sure, with our feeble command and in its present unreliable condition for service it was more than imprudence to tempt fate by throwing it out so far from support. The General intimated he agreed with me, but said Lomax was in a measure under constraint by reason of Early's orders and Rosser's confidence. So we spent the night in our exposed position. At daylight the column was on the move again down the turnpike; it was a foggy morning and you could not see ahead to any extent. We had not proceeded more than a mile or so when our advance commenced firing, and we soon learned we had come in contact with a body of federal cavalry, who had come out to look us up. We met in a position where the turnpike was closed in on either side by hills or woodland, and without hesitation charged the enemy, who gave way, and we followed for some distance, until striking the open country we deployed and went into position. This movement, while necessary and the proper thing under the circumstances, now proved to be the occasion of our undoing, for, as we reached the highland, the mist of the Valley cleared up and our weakness was at once made apparent to our adversaries, who immediately moved to the attack. This attack we withstood for some time; in fact, the men behaved better than we looked for; but in less than an hour's time it became evident we were being overmatched, and our lines began to give away. The advance of the enemy was made in great force, the very ground seemed, as it were, to spew forth cavalry. Every effort was made to retire in order, but the federal advance was so rapid and overwhelming in character that we could not hold together, and by the time Woodstock was reached everything was on the go. The pursuit was maintained for over twenty miles. We lost our guns, and, in fact, everything on wheels. Conspicuous efforts were made to rally and reform, Lomax, Johnson and others exerting themselves to the utmost, but on an attempt to halt and make a stand in a few moments, the charging federal columns on the right and left would dart by and leave you in their lines. McNulty tried hard to save his two guns, but after passing Woodstock his horses gave out and he could go no further. He then unlimbered in the turnpike, charged with cannister, and as I came up he said, "Captain, if you will only get your runaway cavalrymen out of the road I will let into them." At this time the federals had already passed on the west of the pike, and in his front was the confused rabble of our flying people and pursuing federals in one general *melée*. McNulty was forced to quit his guns and tell his men to look out for themselves, and in a moment the guns were in the hands of the enemy. It was said our runaways rode over his men, upsetting the man with friction primers at the lanyard. After this, things generally took their own way. At the "narrow passage" near Edinburg I made an effort to stop, with some ten or twelve men, but a carbine at my head proved an incentive to continue the flight until we reached Mount Jackson. It soon became known that Rosser's experience on the road back was to a degree identical with our own, and Early advanced some infantry from New Market to Rude's hill to stop the flight and the federal advance. The last, however, stopped itself within a few miles of Mount Jackson. That night Lomax came over again, and in deep sorrow and mortification. He asked if any pickets were out, and I told him no; there was no organized command. I went out, however, and gathered together a small party and posted them just below the town. The next day we got together again and found our losses in men and horses were not great, the principal loss being in guns, which were now getting to be a scarce arm in Early's command. It was currently reported some guns sent to Staunton for the army had been marked by a wag, "General Sheridan, care of General Early." Colonel Venable, of General Lee's staff, came up about this time to look around and see what was the matter. He spoke of the state of affairs on the Richmond and Petersburg lines, how they were being held, but with only 1000 men to the mile, and while it was encouraging to know that the undaunted courage and devotion of our comrades was enabling them to make good the defense, yet the information was dispiriting, for it plainly evinced no prospect of the power for any aggressive movement on the part of General Lee, and it was painfully brought home to us that the end was drawing near, when even the present thin lines would become thinner, their defenders fewer and the tactics of extension, which Grant's numbers enabled him to carry out, would result in the final break by reason of the attenuation to which the line was subjected. We talked over the situation, the only relief from which appeared to be the retirement from Richmond and concentration in the interior. With all this, however, there was the supremest trust and confidence that General Lee would do what was proper and right. I fear Colonel Venable did not carry back to his chief anything of comfort, except what could be gained from the spirit manifested by Early in the determination to keep at it as long as he had a force at his command.

The infantry remained at New Market for the next few days, and Lomax, with his division, was sent over to the Page Valley, taking post just below Luray at a point called

Milford. The enemy's cavalry occupied a position immediately in our front and tantalized us by their parades and other evidences of apparent security and comparative comfort, while we threw up such meager defenses as we could and occupied them day and night, being subjected to the constant annoyance of a desultory fire from the opposing lines. Our men suffered for want of regular issues of food, while our poor horses had even a harder time, owing to the absence of grain and long forage. The nights were growing chilly and fires were not allowed on the lines. The federals finally withdrew and we were put into motion for another advance in the direction of Front Royal, it being understood that Early had in contemplation an attack on Sheridan in his entrenched camps at Cedar Creek. Wednesday, October 19th, found us at Front Royal, and from thence we advanced on the Winchester road to within a few miles of that town. During the early morning very heavy firing was heard to our left at Cedar Creek, and Lomax moved in the direction of the main Valley turnpike, and late in the afternoon we reached a position overlooking that road between Middletown and Newtown, very near the point where Jackson struck the retreating columns of Banks in May, 1862, when, to our utter suprise, we found the transportation of Sheridan, instead of hurrying back to Winchester, as expected, was returning toward Middletown. We had heard casually of Early's success in surprising the camps, but there was nothing of a definite character known, and the evidences now presented indicated he had received a check, and as our position was precarious and exposed us to the attack of the superior federal cavalry, Lomax concluded to recross the river and seek a place of safety. In crossing the river that night between Front Royal and Strasburg we fell in with some straggling infantrymen of Kershaw's division, who gave us the intelligence that our forces had met with disaster; so Lomax, without halt, pushed on up the Page Valley and finally rested in our old position near Milford. Then we learned the facts; how that at daylight on the 19th Gordon, supported by Kershaw, had attacked the left of Sheridan's line, driving before him the 8th and 19th corps, taking possession of their camps and forcing back the 6th corps to some distance beyond Middletown, capturing 1300 prisoners and some eighteen pieces of artillery. Owing to the weakness of his force, which was still further depleted by the demoralization incident to such signal success and the inviting plunder offered by the federal camps, Early was not able to continue the advance, neither was much done in the way of securing the fruits of victory. Sheridan was absent from his army at the time, and the news of the disaster which had befallen his command reached him at Winchester as he was returning to the front. Pushing forward with the utmost rapidity, he reached the scene early in the afternoon and immediately took measures to rally his men upon Wright's 6th corps, which had not particularly suffered, and about 4 o'clock made an energetic advance, which could not be stayed by the scattered confederates, at the same time throwing his cavalry forward on his right until they struck Early's rear, capturing wagons and artillery and creating such havoc that another panic or stampede took place, and in a little while the victory of the morning was turned into abject defeat and rout. Early states in his report "It was impossible to rally the troops, the terror of the enemy's cavalry seized them and there was no holding the men." The artillery captured from the enemy in the morning was nearly all recovered by them, together with a number of Early's own guns, and his net loss was twenty-three pieces. About the only organized body that came off was the provost guard, with the 1300 federal prisoners, and Early further states his belief that the imposing appearance of this body, whose identity could not be discovered in the darkness, arrested the federal cavalry and permitted the escape of the army in its routed and demoralized condition. This is the story of the action which has gone down into history, illustrated on canvas and in verse, as "Sheridan's Ride." It was the hardest blow that old Jubal had yet received, and what made it the more mortifying and trying to that able old hero was that a glorious victory, won by his skill and in spite of his feeble numbers, was lost by such misbehavior. In his report to General Lee he very candidly stated all the circumstances and explained the reverse, and concluded in these words: "They are due to no want of effort on my part, though it may be I had not the capacity or judgment to prevent them. I have labored faithfully for success and have not failed to expose my person and set an example to my men, and am still willing to make renewed efforts. If, however, you think the interests of the service would be promoted by a change of commanders I beg you will have no hesitation in making a change." In this action General Ramseur was killed. Early retired to New Market and made effort to reorganize his shattered command. The federal cavalry advanced to Milford, but we repulsed them and held our position.

With this last action closed my experience in the field with the Army of Northern Virginia. In the early part of November a reorganization of the cavalry and a consolidation of the commands took place, and as Johnson was the junior, his brigade was broken up and distributed, and he was ordered to report to the War Department. He had been sent for by General Early at New Market and the situation and the necessity explained, and was made to feel as comfortable as possible under such circumstances. The men of the brigade were from southwest Virginia, as a rule, and in the round up it was natural that officers from that section would have the preference. With the intelligence of the proposed consolidation General Johnson also brought an order for me to report to General Early for assignment to an infantry brigade. This was not altogether in line with my wishes, and particularly at this time when I was suffering from indisposition and felt the need of rest and opportunity to recover my health. To be entirely candid, I was the victim of what was known as the "itch," an ignoble complaint, but a very trying and disagreeable malady to those so afflicted. I did not relish the severing the dear ties of comradeship which I had enjoyed and the casting of my lot with strangers, and on stating my wishes to General Johnson he at once asked that a leave of absence be granted, which was done, and in a few days we both bade fatewell to the cavalry of the Valley District and rode to Charlottesville, General Johnson going to Richmond, while I went to Essex county, on the lower Rappahannock, where I had friends. A few days after we left Sheridan retired from his position, and Early, as usual, advanced to the vicinity of Middletown and Cedar Creek, but finding the enemy still in front of Winchester, returned to New Market, and in December moved back to the railroad, near Fishersville. The country was completely desolated, and no supplies could be had below Staunton. The work of destruction had been faithfully executed, and the Valley no longer afforded subsistence to the confederate; the hungry crow, in truth, carried his rations.

A few weeks' rest and recuperation in Essex made me anxious to return to duty, and in the meantime I heard from General Johnson that he had been assigned to command of the post at Salisbury, N. C., and desired me to report with least possible delay.

1865.

1865.

Salisbury, N. C., at this time was occupied as a prison camp. The advance of Sherman, in his march to the sea, had necessitated the removal of the many prisoners held at various points in the interior to places of safety and the concentration at Salisbury of some 13,000 of these unfortunates. The bringing of so many men to this point in the dead of winter, and without adequate preparation for their care, was the occasion of great suffering and privation. There had previously been established at Salisbury a prison for the confinement of military offenders, with accommodation for some several hundred men, to which our own people, under sentence of courts-martial, were sent for punishment. A stockade had been erected, enclosing a considerable space, including the prison buildings, and into this enclosure were turned the hordes of federal prisoners, with no shelter save an insufficient number of tents. Wood was convenient and in abundant supply; there were also fair water facilities; but an absolute want of proper shelter in this rigorous climate. Officers and enlisted men had been thrown into the confinement indiscriminately, and the result was in December, 1894, an organized effort was made to force the guards, who, in turn, fired into the mob of prisoners with serious effect, killing and wounding a large number. The authorities then took out the officers, and, with the view of ameliorating the condition of the men and of greater security in the now threatened condition of this section, consequent to the near approach of Sherman and the danger from the enterprise of federal cavalry commanders, determined to send an officer from the field to command the post and the district. To this duty General Johnson was assigned, and I reported to him on New Year's day, 1865. Thus opened up my final duty as a confederate soldier and the most painful experience incident to the war. The prison itself was in command of Major Gee, a most estimable gentleman from Florida. He had his headquarters at the prison and took charge of the detail as to discipline, the posting of guards, etc. The troops at the post consisted of several regiments of what were termed "Senior Reserves," that is, North Carolina troops over the age for conscription and active field service, or between forty-five and fifty-five years. With these troops were several officers who had seen field service, but were now retired by reason of wounds or other disability. There were in all, as well as I can remember, some 2500 of these troops, the most miserable, abject specimens of soldiers we had yet fallen in with, with the few exceptions above noted. In addition there was a battalion of "Junior Reserves," or lads between the age of sixteen and eighteen, being below the conscript age. These numbered some 300 perhaps and were worth all the others for efficiency and reliability. One of the companies of this battalion was commanded by a member of the old 1st Maryland Regiment, and it was a reminder of old times to meet him, and through him we soon established good relations with these young warriors. Truly was here exhibited in these troops the straits to which the Confederacy had come —the cradle and the grave were robbed to make good its dire necessities and needs for men. We had our headquarters in the town in a large mansion, which we rented for the purpose. The winter was bitterly cold, but we managed to keep fairly comfortable.

Measures were at once taken to better the condition of the miserable men whom the fortunes of war had thrown on our hands. Method and system were introduced and our meager supplies were made to go as far as human ingenuity could devise. The camp was thoroughly policed and kept clean; the men were encouraged to find occupation; games, etc., were inaugurated, with a view of diverting their attention from their troubles. A thorough system of inspection was established and the weak were protected from the unscrupulous strong. I never before had been confronted with so much abject despair as seemed to pervade these men, and so little of the consideration which comrades usually have one for another. There was a stolidity and absolute indifference that was appalling. The sick received but little attention from their more favored companions, and the dead would lie as they perished until the living were compelled to remove them to the appointed place. Suffering and hopelessness had well-nigh converted many of these men to brutes. I do not record these facts with a disposition to censure or to hold up to blame. They were a motley crowd in the first place, white and black troops huddled together, and the white from almost every nationality under the sun. It was a striking commentary on the character of the material upon which the men of the south were expending themselves. Had these men been like our own people, principally native-born Americans, I am satisfied their behavior and spirits would have better stood the trying ordeal of a prisoner's life. As for food, they were served with the same, in quality and quantity, as the troops who guarded them; that this was slender in supply was their misfortune, not our fault.

When General Johnson arrived and took charge the daily death rate was something frightful, but under the influence of his intelligent and humane administration it was sensibly reduced to more than one-half that which prevailed on our arrival. I found in the prison several Baltimore boys whom I had known well at home; these were paroled and given the liberty of the town, and, as they had good trades, had no difficulty in making a comfortable living.

It is not my purpose to speak of the conditions which led to the suspension of the exchange of prisoners, and which forced upon the confederate authorities the care of so many thousands of federal prisoners when they could illy support and supply with food their own armies in the field. The policy of General Grant and the logic which led him to this position are matters of history. It was hard and trying to the Confederacy, but it was cruel, very cruel, to his own unfortunate men. Justification has been sought in the theory that it was considerate to the living federal that the confederate in a northern prison should be held and not permitted to return to his colors. Such subtle reasoning may have been correct, if we are to ignore all the claims of humanity and subject to our own selfish success the lives and rights of others, but be that as it may, this line of policy prevailed. The poor confederates suffered, languished and died in the northern prison, and in the south the wretched federals were subjected to doubtless greater hardships by reason of the poverty of his captors, while the government for which they had imperiled their lives deliberately permitted them so to suffer and die, unmindful of their misery and cries. There is no phase of the war more dishonoring to the federal arms than the policy they sanctioned, and continued to the very end, regarding prisoners.

After we had things moving in good shape, General Johnson went to Farmville, Va., to spend some little time with Mrs. Johnson, who was stopping at that place. This left on my shoulders the burden of the post and its great responsibilities. About February 1st Governor Vance, of North Carolina, wrote to General Johnson stating most distressing accounts had reached him of the suffering and destitution among the prisoners, which, if true, were a disgrace to our humanity, and offered his aid in making things more tolerable. This letter was received during General Johnson's absence, but I immediately wrote to the Governor, giving a true statement of affairs as we found them on our arrival and the progress we had made in bettering them. The forlorn condition of the prisoners was freely acknowledged, but it was shown we were sharing liberally with them our slender supplies of food, but had no means at hand to provide them with clothing, of which they stood in dire need. It was further stated a full report had been made to the confederate Commissioner of Exchange, Judge Ould, with request that a copy of the report be furnished the federal Commissioner, in order that his government might be officially advised of the character of the privations which their cruel policy was subjecting their unfortunate men in our hands. This correspondence was followed up by General Johnson on his return, and led to federal officers being admitted through our lines with supplies of clothing, which were distributed under their immediate supervision. We had but little meat, and the ordinary substitute, sorghum, was also a scarce commodity; occasionally for several days there could be no issue of the meat ration. The post commissary scoured the country and made every effort to keep up even a meager supply, but without avail, and our own troops were also lacking in this particular. One day in February, after one of these seasons of special scarcity, the Commissary reported to me the arrival at the station of some meat *en route* for General Lee's army, and I gave him the order to take possession of a part of the consignment. What would have been the result of this action had the war lasted much longer I cannot tell; it is mentioned here but to show that not only did we divide what we had with the poor wretches, but even robbed our men in the field. When it is remembered that only a small (about one-third) ration of meat was being issued to the troops in the trenches at Petersburg, and at times no issues were made at all for so long a time as three days, the extent of the consequences of this confiscation may be understood. One good came out of the correspondence with Governor Vance and Judge Ould, and it has always been to me a matter of great satisfaction, that not only did we respond to the utmost to the calls made on our humanity and to do our duty to our fellow-men in these trying experiences, but that our action later on proved to be helpful to a number of brave men whose lives were placed in jeopardy after the surrender, by reason of their connection with the prison service at this point. At the close of the war the enraged sentiment of the north, unmindful of their own record and treatment of confederates who suffered and perished at Johnson's Island, at Camp Chase, Elmira, Point Lookout and other prisons, rose in passionate denouncement of those who controlled the confederate prisons in the south. Officers who had been associated with these prisons were arrested and tried by their modern inquisition, military courts organized to convict, and one poor fellow, Captain Wirz, the commandant at Andersonville, was hanged to satisfy the demand for a victim. Major Gee, our commandant at Salisbury, together with

Major Myers, the Commissary, and perhaps others, were also subjected to arrest, but fortunately for them the correspondence in question was produced in evidence and they were released. Major Myers assured me that it would have gone hard with them but for the facts which were presented so candidly and the evidence of our purpose to do the best for our charge the limited means at our disposal would admit.

After my return home I had repeated voluntary offers from men who were in the prison and who appreciated our efforts in their behalf to testify if needed. It was an inglorious duty which fell to our lot, full of sadness and trial, but, under a merciful Providence, we saw our duty and had the disposition and opportunity of materially lessening the distress and suffering around us. While I claim no special credit for what was done, yet I have been ever thankful for the opportunity of rendering service to these miserable unfortunates who were, by the fate of war and the callous indifference of their own government, called to undergo so painful an experience.

Prison duty, with all its distresses, had its humors. Major Gee was accustomed to call at headquarters early every morning and make report of the events of the preceding day and night. On the occasion of one of my visits to the prison I was walking with him on the parapet or platform on the outer side of the fence or stockade, and on which the sentries were posted, when he said to me in an undertone, "Do not stop, but just below where we now are is a tunnel in course of construction; I know all about it, but propose to allow them to continue the work, and have arranged to meet them as they break through on the outside." The Major thought it wise to allow the poor devils to enjoy the "pleasure of hope" and thus keep their minds and bodies employed, at the same time his duty required him to prevent escapes. One of the most heartless conditions of the prison was the ready ease and facility with which some of the prisoners would communicate to the commandant the doings of their comrades, hoping to gain some personal favor as a reward for their vile conduct. I had frequently discussed this situation with Major Gee from an ethical standpoint, and he was of the opinion that it was all right to avail himself of such means of information, although I will do him the justice to say he did not voluntarily suggest or encourage it. He frequently told me the information came freely, without making it necessary for him to specially solicit such traitorous conduct.

This particular engineering party who were delving in the ground, with his knowledge, were to break through on a certain night, of which he also was informed. He stationed a company of our "Senior Reserves," so as to take care of the men as they came to the surface, some fifteen or twenty feet beyond the enclosure. The officer in charge watched through the night, and as day approached with no evidence of ground-breaking, he concluded it not worth while to stay until relieved or ordered back, and so marched his men away. Shortly after his departure the break was made, and when it became fully day it was seen the effort had been successful, and in calling the rolls in the prison it was found a dozen or more men had made good their escape. This intelligence was conveyed to the astonished commandant, who posted up to headquarters at once and roused me out of my blankets with the startling intelligence that, after all his foreknowledge and care, he had been outwitted by reason of the blundering stupidity of the officer in charge of his guard. I laughed most heartily, and soon all of us were guying the irate Major. Frankly, we hoped the poor fellows would get away, but as duty required, we took steps for their apprehension. Most of them were recaptured, but a few made good their escape into western North Carolina, in which section they found friends and shelter until they could cross into east Tennessee.

We had about headquarters an Irishman taken from the prison; he cooked and did chores for us and was a very handy fellow. He claimed to have been a soldier in the regular army, but, immediately before enlisting in the war, had been employed as coachman by Governor Morgan, of New York. He became very much attached to me and was quite obliging. I do not believe he would have left us willingly, but when the final arrangements were made to exchange or return the prisoners we sent him off with them. He offered to call on my family in Baltimore with messages, and I gave him the address. After reaching home I learned he had been as good as his word, and he had regaled them with the most remarkable accounts of my position and services, and told of incidents that shocked my dear old grandmother very much, until it was suggested by some of the family that the fellow was drawing a long bow. He really intended it all in kindness, and thought it would be most grateful to them to know that the cadet of the house was such a rollicking soldier of the O'Malley type.

One morning I was escorting through the prison Major Hall, of the A. & I. General Office, who had been sent from Richmond to inspect the post. Major Gee was, of course, doing the honors and explaining the manner in which the prisoners lived and passed away their time. Owing to the want of sufficient tents, many of them had constructed shelters by burrowing in the ground to some extent, and, utilizing cracker boxes and refuse lumber, made sort of dug-outs, in which they lived like so many rabbits. Major Hall was much interested, but very indignant that their necessities should compel such crude makeshifts; his sensibilities were destined to receive a much ruder shock. As we were passing a low shed-like structure, Major Gee invited him to enter. It was the deadhouse. Every morning developed that a number had died during the night, and they were at once conveyed to this building, where the bodies were laid in a row, until arrangement could be made for interment. The deaths at this time were about thirty per day. Here was now a long row of the dead before us; white and black lay side by side. Major Gee remarked, "Like Saul and Jonathan, lovely in life, in death they are not divided." The horrors of the scene had seriously affected Major Hall, a gentleman of the highest sensibility and culture, and this casual remark from Major Gee struck him with particular offense, and I remember to this moment the expression of disgust on his countenance as he turned and walked away, and his subsequent denunciation of what appeared to him to be utter heartlessness. I explained to him, as we returned to town, that he was much mistaken in Major Gee, who was a gentleman, as himself, of culture and fine feeling, but the constant contact with these terrible experiences had worn off the horrifying influences, and that in true humanity, sympathy and effort to relieve suffering Major Gee was diligent day and night. As bad as things were at this time, to those whose knowledge extended back to the period when they were so much worse, the condition appeared to be almost satisfactory, at least relatively so. In March the efforts to restore the prisoners to their friends began to bear fruit, and instructions were received to forward them to the seaboard near Wilmington. I know the poor fellows were not more glad to go than we were to be relieved of their charge. As we had only limited transportation on the railroads, the trains could only be used as helpers; that is, the cars would be filled and moved a distance on the way and then emptied and returned for another load, thus alternating with the marching column and giving such assistance as was possible. It was a difficult matter to get together supplies sufficient to give the men several days' issue of rations, but by hard work we finally got the prison cleared. As the prisoners approached the federal lines near the coast they were held up, as I understand, for several days before the federal commander would permit them to come in, and this during a fearful storm, which added to the suffering and caused loss of life. Some misunderstanding of a technical character now made this last experience of these poor men, inflicted by their own people, even more trying than the trials they had encountered and undergone with us. One of my Baltimore *protégés* died on the trip on his way homeward, the result of this severe exposure.

It had become painfully evident within the past few weeks that the end was at hand. Sherman was moving up through the State, and the news from General Lee's army indicated that he would not be able to hold on to the Richmond lines much longer. General Johnson and myself discussed the situation very freely, and also met Mr. Stephens, the Vice-President, on his way to his home in Georgia. Mr. Stephens gave an account of his mission, together with Mr. Hunter and Judge Campbell, to meet Mr. Lincoln at Fort Monroe, and remarked that he was now going home to tell his people they had nothing further to expect save from some miraculous interposition in their favor, as there were no terms to be made. It has been frequently charged that Mr. Davis and other confederate leaders were criminal in not recognizing the inevitable as now presented, and that their determination to continue the struggle was the result of apprehension as to their personal safety, and fear of the consequences from this selfish standpoint. The heroic nature of Jefferson Davis is not open to such reflection. Had he been convinced that duty to his people required that the Confederacy should have abandoned the contest, I have no doubt he would have led the way, without one thought of the consequences to himself, but would have offered the sacrifice, even had his life been the price to pay for peace. His chivalric spirit rose and the nobility of his soul asserted itself just in proportion as the outward circumstances became more unpromising. Again, the army, depleted as it was, its ranks thinned by battle and intense suffering, would not have listened to any composition while the remotest opportunity existed for maintaining the struggle. The great questions involved in this war were only to be settled by the absolute exhaustion and inability to continue the contest of one or the other of the high parties. So long as there was a confederate army extant, so long would the fight be waged. The battle color of the Confederacy was not to be furled as long as there was a hand to wave it or a gun to protect it; when these failed, and then only, was it to be laid to rest. It was best for the country, the great American republic of the future, and for the generations to come, that this fight for principle should be fought out to the finish, and it was so recognized by General Lee, who did not intimate his willingness to consider the proposition to lay down arms until the Army of Northern Virginia found itself hemmed in on every side, with but 8000 half-starved, worn and weary men with arms who could form line of battle against the overwhelming forces of Grant, that the futility of further opposition and the duty to stop further effusion of blood was recognized.

After the prisoners had been dispatched our occupation at Salisbury was in a measure gone. In going to Salisbury I had left my horse in Virginia to recruit. Now that the spring campaign was about to open up, I received leave of absence to go to Essex to get my mount. I passed through Richmond on April 2d, Saturday, the day before the lines were broken in front of Petersburg. There was but little evidence of the impending calamity; it was true the firing on the lines was heavy, but that had become to be an every-day occurrence and excited no particular comment. I called upon my tailor and paid him for an undress uniform coat, $1200, giving him in payment a $20 gold piece, at the current rate of exchange, sixty for one, with the privilege of redeeming the same on my return. I was rather short of confederate money at the time, but thought it best under the circumstances to close my account. I reached Essex late in the night, after a ride of nearly sixty miles. On Monday morning I was awakened by the servants, who were loudly talking at the wood-pile near the house, and on enquiry as to the occasion of their chattering and excitement, was informed that news had arrived that Richmond had been "evaccinated." Immediately after breakfast I rode out in search of news, and to my sorrow found plenty of corroborative testimony. The next day a federal gunboat came up the river and communicated with the shore, confirming the sad tidings. There were in the neighborhood several soldiers, at home on leave, and we at once consulted as to our future course. While waiting for tidings of the army, came the heartrending intelligence from Appomattox, and then the cup of our misery and sorrow overflowed. Words cannot describe the feelings of the confederate soldier when it was brought home to him that, after the struggles and sacrifices of four long years, his noble chieftain had yielded to the influences he was no longer able to withstand, and that the Army of Northern Virginia had passed into history. Strong men wept, and despair seemed to take hold of all. There was not one word of murmuring or adverse criticism; the grief was too pronounced and the dismay too appalling. Then came the conviction that if General Lee thought it was best his decision must be accepted. Then followed a ray of dim hope—Johnston was yet in the field, and we conjured up the possibilities from this consideration. We mapped out all sorts of campaigns and plans, and then determined to get together a party and make our way to join the new paladin of our hopes.

The day we met at our *rendezvous* for this movement this last ray of promise faded, as the report reached us that Johnston had likewise surrendered to Sherman. In a little while federal troops established themselves through the country, and proclamation was made for all soldiers to come forward and be paroled. I had now occasion to visit Richmond, and found no difficulty in entering the city, passing through the federal outposts without hindrance, but found that exit from the city was not quite so easy, and required a permit from the Provost-Marshal. The main portion of the city was in ruins from the fire, but the heroic citizens were exerting themselves to map out some line of action and policy for the future. It was now admitted on all hands that the war was over. All further resistance was at an end, and our leading men counselled obedience to authority and law.

On going to the office of the Provost for permission to pass through the picket, I was informed it would be necessary to be first paroled, and to this I assented, and gave to the officer my name and rank, whereupon he immediately questioned me as to any possible relationship to J. Wilkes Booth. I disclaimed any connection with the assassin of Mr. Lincoln, and remarked that it occurred to me to be a very unnecessary question, as it was scarcely probable I would acknowledge a relationship under existing circumstances even if it were true in fact. He smiled, and after a few more enquiries handed me my parole, signed by D. M. Evans, Col. and P. M. This document gave me permission to go to my "home" in Essex county and there remain undisturbed so long as I obeyed the laws, etc. I had given Essex as my home, for what could a poor Marylander now claim? The rampant and violent spirit which was in the ascendency in Maryland at once began to refuse asylum to those of her sons who had served in the armies of the Confederacy, and the few who had already returned met with abuse and maltreatment. For some little while vindictiveness and passion held sway, but soon other and more considerate influences came to the front, and particularly efficacious in this connection was the interpretation placed by General Grant on the terms of the surrender, and his counsel to encourage all confederates to resume their peaceful vocations without let or hindrance.

The generosity of General Grant's nature in his dealing with the confederate soldier now became the marked characteristic of his true greatness. His wisdom and foresight took in the future and recognized a reunited country, which was now but on the threshold of its fame and coming greatness—a country in which the development of the south and the support of its sons would be as marked and as dearly prized as the much-boasted loyalty of their northern brethren. He discouraged oppression, pains and penalties. "Let us have peace" was his utterance, and upon this will his fame rest more securely even than his military successes. It is true he was unable entirely to withstand the demands of party and the violence of the demagogues, but as he became more experienced in political matters, and neared the end of his career, he grew stronger in these convictions of liberality and just dealing. For these kindnesses, for the courtesy to our noble Lee, and other evidences of moderation, considerateness and manliness, the living confederate of today honors his memory.

In the early part of June I received intelligence that the way was now clear to return to Baltimore, and, after an absence of our four years, I found myself again with loved and dear ones.

My old grandfather, himself a soldier of 1812-14, insisted, however, I should go with him to the office of the Provost-

Marshal, register and take the oath of allegiance to the United States, which being done I ceased to be a confederate soldier on parole and became a restored citizen of our great republic. It took considerable time to recount the experiences of the past to eager and sympathetic ears, and in turn to hear from those at home the story of their trials and the indignities to which they had been subjected. The Union population of Maryland were afflicted during the war with a species of loyal rabies, and their passion and this malignant malady expended itself even on the children, if so be they unfortunately displayed the southern colors, red and white. In all the border States and divided communities this vindictiveness found expression, but, thank God, today finds us with the absence of this feeling, and, instead, as true and united a people and as devoted to our common country as any State within the Union.

The memories of the past survive, the associations of old times are maintained, and the truth of history is being preserved, but the animosities of the past are gone, and we have learned and are still learning to respect the motives of each other, while the gallantry of the sons of Maryland, whether they followed the cross of the Confederacy under Lee, Jackson or Johnson, or loyally supported the stars and stripes under Grant and Sherman, remain the proud heritage of our loved Commonwealth.

The results of the war were far-reaching; the question of the permanence of the Union was settled for all time; but the cause of the Confederacy, in so far as it represented the principles of liberty, home rule and the rights of the States, was not lost. They remain and abide with us today, supported and maintained by our federal courts, and find their resting place in the hearts of all people, north as well as south.

The institution of slavery, and for which the people of the south were not responsible, perished among the things ignoble; the true, the good and the best remain. The phenomenal development of the south, the wonderful industry of her people in restoring waste places and overcoming the desolations of the war, the forebearance with which they continued to strive under a political oppression of the most violent type, until the good sense and the great heart of the people rose in protest, are matters of history, and today, thirty-three years after Lee furled his banner at Appomattox, the country is entering upon a foreign war, the men of the north and the men of the south, side by side, at the bidding of a country stronger for its past differences and trials, and Lee and Wheeler, who led the horse of the Confederacy in Virginia and in the west, are now wearing the blue in command of federal troops, under the starry banner of our own great and united country. "Truly God moves in mysterious ways."

And now my tale is done. These pages, far more drawn out and extended than I had intended at the outset, are devoid of literary merit and entirely without any effort to display. I have told a plain unvarnished story; what is lacking in style may, I trust, find compensation in the fairness and absolute truthfulness of the facts and figures. I have spoken of things as I saw them, without malice and free from passion or fear. If I have overstepped the bounds of modest propriety, or grown prosy and uninteresting, this must be ascribed to the natural garrulity of an old soldier in fighting over his battles. That I view my participation in the stirring events herein narrated with some pride is freely admitted, and, in conclusion, I confidently assert I would not part with my own inconsiderable share of the glories of the Army of Northern Virginia for a fortune of wealth. My chief and only regret arises from the poverty and insignificance of my service, where there was so much of greatness and so much of glory.

G. W. BOOTH.

www.ingramcontent.com/pod-product-compliance
Lightning Source LLC
Chambersburg PA
CBHW032155160426
43197CB00008B/920